Life After
Phillip Morris

STEVEN RUSSELL

Life After Phillip Morris

STEVEN RUSSELL

WITH
LAURENCE WATTS

CAUTION

CONTENTS

FOREWORD

STEVEN RUSSELL ENTERED MY LIFE on Saturday, September 5, 2009. That was the date *The Observer*, the left-of-center British newspaper, published a long article by Elizabeth Day titled *I Love You Phillip Morris: A Conman's Story*. Steven's story transfixed me.

Here was a man who had successfully lied, swindled and tricked his way through life. Who had convinced a billion-dollar company to appoint him its CFO in spite of his criminal record and the fact he knew nothing about accounting. Who had escaped prison a total of four times, yet never once climbed over a high fence topped with razor wire. This guy, I reasoned, was a genius. Best of all, if Day's account of Russell's life was to be believed, he did it all for love. "The love that dare not speak its name" as Wilde famously termed it.

Aside from his exploits, intelligence and sexuality however, the detail of Steven's life that captured my imagination most was the fact he was serving a 144-year sentence for cumulative non-violent crime. That seemed absurd.

I'm not a great believer in prison as a method for punishing individuals. For me, prisons should exist to protect law-abiding citizens from unrepentant lawbreakers. Where wrongs have been committed, I believe in restitution for victims at the wrongdoers' expense, much as occurs under civil law. As such, I fail to see how the present system of widespread incarceration benefits anyone. In Steven Russell's case, what possible risk did he pose to society? What was the point of keeping him behind bars? The only risk Steven posed was to the prison officials from whom he might escape. And the surest and cheapest way of protecting their pride and job security would be to release him. To me, his ongoing incarceration was and is outrageous.

Six months after reading his *Observer* interview, I saw the film *I Love You Phillip Morris* on the opening night of its release at a packed Greenwich Arts Cinema, in Southeast London. I have never laughed so hard watching a film. By my reckoning, Jim Carrey gives the best performance of his career as Steven, while Ewan McGregor is equally compelling as his boyfriend, Phillip. The film was clever, playful and side-splittingly funny. That its two main characters are gay is gloriously irrelevant to the plot.

Just under a year later, I started writing features for the British publication *Pink News*. Typically this involved me talking to and profiling leading figures from the global LGBT community. Throughout 2011, I interviewed the likes of Lt. Dan Choi, Peter Tatchell, Perez Hilton, Bishop Gene Robinson, RuPaul and CNN's Don Lemon, to name just a few. One of the things I liked best about my 'job' was that I got to meet a great number of my personal heroes. With a dozen or so interviews under my belt, I decided to approach Steven Russell. I figured the worst that could happen was he would say no. I tracked Steven down to the Texas Department of Criminal Justice's (TDCJ) Michael Unit in Tennessee Colony and on August 10, I wrote him a letter asking for an interview. I heard nothing back.

Little did I know, but the TDCJ had just decided to transfer Steven from the Michael Unit to the Allan B. Polunsky Unit, some ninety-two miles south. Looking back, the convoy transporting Steven probably crossed paths with my letter somewhere on the I-45. When mail addressed to his former prison was eventually forwarded to him, Steven responded and agreed to be interviewed via exchange-of-letters. The two of us corresponded for some weeks and our resulting interview was published on October 21, 2011.

Corresponding with Steven only fueled my interest in him. I now wanted to know what happened next in his story, and I had a feeling that others who had seen *I Love You Phillip Morris* did too. That's when I suggested he and I might write a sequel to the film, and the book upon which it is based. Steven was interested, but insisted on meeting me in person before committing his time and energy. That necessitated me making a trip to Texas.

I was living in San Diego, California when the time came for my visit. I made the 1,300-mile road trip to Texas over two long days of driving, arriving at the Polunsky Unit, near Livingston, on Sunday, February 12, 2012. It was the first time I'd ever set foot inside a prison.

For a man who had been subject to solitary confinement since 1998 (almost 20 years at the time of writing) Steven was remarkably engaging, funny and kind. Re-reading Elizabeth Day's *Observer* piece now makes me realize how similar our experiences of meeting Steven were, in spite of the fact they occurred at two different TDCJ facilities.

Having made my way through security, I found my way to the prison's visitation room. There I was allocated a numbered booth, where I sat and waited patiently for Steven to arrive. Ten to fifteen minutes later he was escorted to me, his hands cuffed behind his back. He seemed happy to see me and very much used to prison procedures. I was not. Dressed in a white prison uniform, he sat down in a chair on his side of a dividing Plexiglas screen and we conversed via telephone. Prior to our meeting, the only picture I'd seen of Steven was one taken by a local photographer, George Hixson, in 1997, which had appeared in *The Observer*. In the flesh, Steven was a little plumper than I had expected. I guess three meals a day and solitary confinement would eventually do that to a guy.

We laughed as I told him more about me. I bought him snacks from some nearby vending machines and asked him some basic questions about his life. Before our allotted two hours were up, Steven told me he'd be happy to write this book. The story would be his, hence the designation 'By Four-Time Prison Escapee Steven Russell'. My role would be to shape and embellish the tale, guiding him towards what I thought the public wanted to know.

Why make *Life After Phillip Morris* a play? Well, Steven's life since his last arrest, in 1998, has more or less been lived in the small concrete box that constitutes his cell and world. It is a life that has principally been lived alone. I worried that a straight autobiography about a man who doesn't move about or interact much with others would come across as too dry. Instead, I sold Steven on the idea of updating his story in play form because, not only would that allow it to be performed, it would also give us some artistic license in how we explained the last twenty years of his life.

As such, *Life After Phillip Morris* is 'based on a true story', which is to say that although almost all the events detailed in this book happened, they didn't necessarily take place in the order in which we tell them. Moreover, some of the characters in the play exist in real life while others do not. For the real people we portray, you should take it as read that, Steven aside, any views they express in *Life After Phillip Morris* are not their own. Furthermore, Gabriel Unit, the location in which the play is set, represents an amalgam of prisons in which Steven has been housed over the years.

Although the play raises some serious issues, it is primarily meant to entertain. When I first told Steven that I wanted to make *Life After Phillip Morris* a comedy, I worried he would think I wasn't taking him seriously. I needn't have been concerned. He agreed with the premise wholeheartedly. Luckily for me, Steven's humor is much like my own: self-deprecating, coarse, colorful and with scant regard for political correctness.

My motivation in co-writing this book is to highlight that Steven's life didn't end when moviegoers walked out of the theater at the end of *I Love You Phillip Morris*. His life continued afterwards, it continues to this day, and it is criminal - no pun intended - that he remains behind bars when he has never physically harmed another human being.

I would like to thank a number of people for helping me co-write this book. The first, of course, is Steven himself. I would also like to thank John Requa and Glenn Ficarra, the directors of *I Love You Phillip Morris*, for sharing the story of how their film was made. Additional thanks go to Brian Groff who took the photograph for the front cover and Sophie Cutner and Stephen Gray for their perspectives.

Laurence Watts
July 2018

CAST

IN ORDER OF APPEARANCE

Major Linke	A prison guard at Gabriel Unit
Steven Russell	A conman and serial prison escapist
Lt. Herrera	A Latino prison guard at Gabriel Unit
Narrator	A future version of Steven Russell
Warden Alvarado	The warden of Gabriel Unit
Media Relations Officer	A female Gabriel Unit employee
Steve McVicker	A journalist with *The Houston Journal*
Prisoner	A blond-haired male prisoner
Barney	An inmate in Gabriel Unit
Kelly	Another inmate in Gabriel Unit
Sally	Steven Russell's daughter
Beautiful Woman	A beautiful woman
John Requa	A Hollywood screenwriter and director
Glenn Ficarra	A Hollywood screenwriter and director
Diana Knight	A freelance journalist from Britain
Double	A figment of someone's imagination

STAGE PLAN

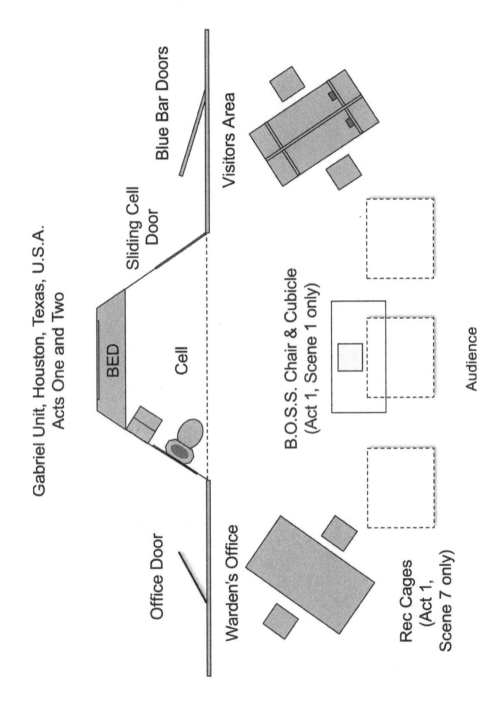

ACT ONE

SCENE ONE

The CURTAIN *rises to reveal a processing room in the Texas Department of Criminal Justice's (TDCJ) Gabriel Unit, Houston. A curtain cubicle stands center stage, much like those that wrap around hospital beds. It is illuminated from within. In the center of the cubicle is a chair.*

Three men walk on from stage right: Major Linke, Steven Russell and Lt. Herrera. Major Linke and Lt. Herrera are dressed in blue, police-like uniforms, while Steven wears what looks like an orange jumpsuit but is in fact a prison-issued orange shirt and matching pants.

Steven is shackled by handcuffs, which are attached by a chain to manacles around his ankles. The connecting chain is not quite long enough to allow him to stand upright; as such, he stands and walks a little hunched over. The three men walk into the cubicle and are cast in silhouette.

The date is early April 1998. Unless stated, everyone has Texan accents.

Major Linke stands to the left of the chair, while Steven and Lt. Herrera stand to the chair's right.

Major Linke: Remove the shackles from the prisoner!

Lt. Herrera begins the process of removing Steven's manacles. It is a slow process

11

that begins at his feet and continues thereon upwards as the relevant key is found and each lock is carefully undone.

Lt. Herrera (*with a Hispanic accent*): If you try anything, Russell, I'm gonna Mace you. You got that?

Steven: I'm too tired to try anything. It's been a long day.

Major Linke (*to Steven*): Stop running your mouth!

We hear the clinking of metal. Steven co-operates with the process. After a brief moment the Narrator enters stage right, walks to front of the stage and addresses the audience. The Narrator is wearing a dark blue suit, white shirt and pink tie.

Narrator (*cheerfully*): Well, there you all are! Hello, good evening and welcome all you lucky, discerning and, dare I say it, handsome people.

Steven (*to Major Linke and Lt. Herrera*): Who the fuck is that?

Major Linke (*firmly*): Zip it!

Narrator (*eccentrically*): My name is Steven Russell.

Steven: That's my name!

Lt. Herrera: Will you shut up?

Narrator (*continuing*): ... and I will be your narrator for tonight's performance of *Life After Phillip Morris*.

Steven (*to Major Linke and Lt. Herrera*): You guys can't hear that?

Major Linke: All I hear is you whining like a bitch.

Narrator (*still to the audience*): Please take a moment to locate and note the position of your nearest emergency exit so that, in the event of fire, you can have more time to trample the person sitting next to you as we all rush to get the fuck out of here!

In the event of a loss of cabin pressure oxygen masks will fall down from the ceiling. The flow of oxygen can be activated by swiping your credit card through the card-reader hidden behind your tray table. Please affix your own mask before assisting others. If you're travelling with two or more children, please decide in advance which one of the two you love the most.

Steven (*confused*): Is there a television on out there or something?

Lt. Herrera (*to Steven*): Quit acting up or I'll start putting these back on!

Narrator: The play you are about to watch is all about me!

He grins from ear to ear, before his grin fades and he points to Steven.

But unfortunately it's also about him. The one in chains, that is, not one of the two boneheads either side of him. You see, he's also Steven Russell.

Steven (*to Major Linke and Lt. Herrera, still confused*): You guys really don't hear that?

Major Linke (*to Steven*): If you don't settle down, I will gas you!

Narrator: So, in summary: he's me and I'm him. He's younger, but I'm prettier. The longer you laugh by the way the longer I have to hold this smile. So, questions. Who is Steven Russell? Who is Phillip Morris? Where are we? When are we?

The Narrator begins pacing back and forth across the front of the stage.

It's April 1998. President Bill Clinton is in his second term, someone called George W. Bush is currently Governor of Texas, and NASA has just announced there's enough water on the moon to support a human colony. *Titanic* has just won Best Picture at the 70th Academy Awards, but Will Smith's *Gettin Jiggy Wit It* has thankfully just knocked *My Heart Will Go On* from the top of the Billboard 100.

He points at Steven.

This man, Steven Russell, has just been arrested in Florida and, would you believe, flown back here to Houston, Texas, at the taxpayers' expense aboard the state's private plane!

Firstly, who even knew that Texas had its own plane? Secondly, what kind of a man are we dealing with here? He looks kind of dangerous, right? With all the chains and stuff? Is he a mafia boss? (*Pause*) The head of an international drug syndicate? (*Pause*) Maybe he's a terrorist?

Well, he's none of those. But so embarrassing are his crimes to the state of Texas that, while the press were told he'd be landing at Houston Intercontinental Airport and there would be a press conference relating to his arrest... that was all a decoy. He was actually flown straight here via a nearby airstrip. Sucks to be a member of the press, eh?

So, where is here? This is the Texas Department of Criminal Justice's Gabriel Unit. It's a prison, and it's here that Texas houses its death-row inmates: the most dangerous people in the whole of the state, outside of the Governor's mansion.

How many people did Steven Russell kill? None. He's not a killer. Did he blow up a government building? No. Did he physically harm any individual? No.

Steven Russell is nothing more than a con artist with a fondness for long walks and fresh air. Why is he here? Well, prison isn't such a great place for someone who likes walking. Cell bars, walls and fences tend to get in the way. So, pursuing his hobby sometimes means walking out the prison's front door. Which we did four times.

Inside the cubicle Steven is now free of his manacles. Major Linke continues the process.

Major Linke (*to Steven*): Come out of your shoes.

Steven Russell complies with the instruction and removes his shoes, handing each one to Lt. Herrera.

Narrator (*continuing*): Now I can see how the uninitiated might confuse such harmless rambling with, say, escaping from prison, but they are missing an important point! We were always planning on coming back... If they found us.

You see, in addition to a fondness for walking, Steven and I are also very keen hide-and-seek players. And we especially like playing hide-and-seek after a nice long walk.

Major Linke (*issuing another order*): Give me your socks.

Steven complies, handing his socks one by one to Lt. Herrera.

Lt. Herrera: Man, they stink! When was the last time you changed them?

Steven (*indifferently*): About a week ago.

Narrator: So, hopefully, you can see it was only by accident that we got labelled 'the most prolific prison escaper in Texas' history.' It's all just one big misunderstanding.

Major Linke (*to Steven*): Give me your shirt.

Narrator: Now you'd think escaping prison would be difficult, right? Well, let me let you in on a little secret: IT IS!!! Prisons are designed to keep people in. They have locks and razor wire, guard towers and electric fences, searchlights and guards with guns. Escaping from prison is pretty difficult. Moreover, breaking out of jail is even harder when you're known to have escaped once, twice or three times before.

Major Linke (*to Steven*): Give me your pants and boxers.

Steven Russell complies handing his pants and eventually his shorts to Lt.

Herrera. He is now naked, though the audience can only see his silhouette.

Narrator: Now, I'm guessing some of you are wondering what's going on in there. Let me explain. Having been apprehended after escaping prison for the fourth time, I'm being processed before being taken to my new cell. In due course I'll be convicted and sentenced for this latest escapade, but for now they're just going to lock me up again since I was already serving 65 years for escape and aggregate theft. Aggregate theft, by the way, doesn't mean that I used force or held up a bank with a gun. It just means I wasn't keen on giving back the money I'd stolen.

Now, the interesting thing is: this isn't a prison I've escaped from before. This one's new to me. I suppose that fourth escape, which was my most audacious, was the straw that broke the camel's back.

Now they're going to keep me in administrative segregation with the Texas death-row inmates. As I'm sure you can guess, that's pretty much the most secure wing of any jail in Texas. They clearly don't want me to go wandering off again.

Interestingly, they're actually going to subject me to greater security than the murderers on death row. I'm going to be watched continuously, my cell will be searched regularly and I'm going to be rotated to a different cell every few days. They think this will save them any future embarrassment. They're wrong.

Major Linke: Sit in the B.O.S.S. chair and raise your left arm.

Steven Russell does as he is told and Lt. Herrera waves a metal-detector over and around his extended arm.

Narrator: The first time I escaped from prison was on March 13, 1992. I was doing some time in Harris County Jail for some light insurance fraud, and in the meantime the love of my life was dying from AIDS.

Major Linke: Lower your left arm and raise your right arm.

Steven complies and Lt. Herrera waves the metal-detector around his right arm.

Narrator: Did I mention that I'm gay? The tie gave it away, right? Or was it the lover dying of AIDS? Anyway, had I stayed put and served my time like a good little boy, Jimmy, my lover, would have been dead by the time I got out. The way I saw it, he needed someone to take care of him and I sure as hell wanted to spend as much time with him while we still could.

So, I started studying the prison and its guards. The visitors' area seemed to me to be the chink in their armor and one that I decided to exploit. I got a job as a trusty, an inmate who helps with prison administration, and used the freedom it gave me to acquire a t-shirt, a pair of red sweatpants and a walkie-talkie. I stashed them with a young offender called Chris until I needed them. He was housed in a holding cell outside of general population.

Major Linke (*to Steven*): Lower your right arm and raise your left leg.

Lt. Herrera scans Steven's left leg.

Narrator: When the time was right, I collected my stuff from Chris, changed out of my prison uniform and into the t-shirt and sweatpants. I walked up to the nearest guard's picket and tapped on the window with the walkie-talkie. They mistook me for an undercover police officer and opened the door for me. I walked into the prison's visitors' area and out into the world via the visitors' entrance and parking lot. In other words, I literally walked out of the front door!

Major Linke: Put your left leg down and raise your right leg.

Steven: Are we doing the hokey dokey?

Lt. Herrera: Russell, I won't tell you again.

Lt. Herrera scans his right leg.

Narrator (*excitedly*): Those first moments of freedom felt amazing!

Like your first gulp of iced water after you've been outside in 100-degree heat. Only combine that with an adrenaline rush that leaves you dizzy to the point of blacking out! My heart felt like it was exploding in my chest. But the best thing was, I knew I would get to see Jimmy and take care of him.

He lived for another 26 months after my escape and I managed to spend most of that time with him. A few weeks before he died though, I was back in custody after the police finally caught up with me in Philadelphia. It had taken them more than two years to track me down.

Major Linke: Put your right leg down and open your mouth, tongue down.

Lt. Herrera: Say 'ah'!

Lt. Herrera peers into Steven's mouth.

Steven: Ah.

Narrator: My second escape took place in July 1996. By then I'd met Phillip Morris in the prison law library while serving out the time I had left for my insurance conviction. Phillip was in for automobile-related theft.

I took Jimmy's death pretty hard, but by the time I met Phillip I was ready to love again. And boy did I fall in love! When Phillip and I were both paroled at the end of 1995 we set about building a life together.

Lt. Herrera (*to Major Linke*): Nothing.

Major Linke (*to Steven*): Raise your tongue to the roof of your mouth.

Lt. Herrera: Say 'ah' again.

Steven: Ah again.

Narrator: Being the alpha of the relationship, it became my responsibility to keep Phillip and me in a lifestyle to which we were unaccustomed. That meant earning some serious cash. The only trouble was, companies weren't keen on hiring ex-cons for anything other than menial work. Well, that simply wasn't going to pay the bills.

So, I decided to employ some creative writing and falsify my references and resume. Bingo! Not long after, I got a job as the Chief Financial Officer of a health management organization called North American Medical Management, or NAMM for short.

Major Linke (*to Steven*): Close your mouth and lift up your penis.

Steve: Do you want it to say 'ah' too?

Narrator: In the four months that I worked for NAMM, I managed to steal $800,000 before I was eventually caught.

Let me put that another way. It took them four months to realize I had no qualifications, no experience and had never worked in finance or healthcare before. That's sixteen weeks of meetings, working nine-to-five, conference calls and one-on-ones.

In the end I was charged with aggregate theft. Can you believe it? They put a convicted felon in charge of their finance department. They should have been charged with incitement!

Major Linke (*to Steven*): Pull back your foreskin.

Steven (*to Linke*): I'm cut, you goddamn idiot!! Are you even watching this?

Major Linke: Lift up your penis and balls, and spread your cheeks so we know there's nothing up your ass.

Steven complies.

Narrator: Anyway, by July 1996, I was back behind bars and getting close to trial. I was looking at a forty-five-year sentence for the NAMM theft. Forty-five years! I didn't have time for that. I had things to do and places to be.

So, I called up the district clerk's office using a prison phone, impersonated a judge and reduced my bail amount from $900,000 to $45,000, which I then arranged to be paid. And once again, I walked out of the prison's front door a free man.

Well, free until I missed the trial hearing they expected me to attend. Like I was ever going to show up for that! But they caught up with me again, this time in less than five days.

Major Linke (*to Lt. Herrera*): Can you see anything?

Lt. Herrera (*crouched down and looking at Steven's asshole*): Maybe. I don't know.

Major Linke: Fine, we'll do it the easy way. (*To Steven*) Stand up, turn around, bend over and spread your ass cheeks.

Narrator (*acknowledging what's happening behind him*): They like their nudity here at the Gabriel Unit.

Steven complies with Major Linke's order.

Major Linke (*to Lt. Herrera*): Well?

Lt. Herrera hasn't moved.

Lt. Herrera: Well, what?

Major Linke: Do you see anything?

Lt. Herrera: I'm not going anywhere near that thing. You should have smelled his socks!

Major Linke (*raising his voice*): Lieutenant, does the prisoner have anything concealed in his ass?

Lt. Herrera cautiously moves in for a closer inspection.

Lt. Herrera (*jumping back*): Jesus Christ!!!

Major Linke (*alarmed*): What is it?

Steven: I farted.

Major Linke: Russell!

Steven: I'm sorry, but if you ask me to bend over and open my butthole... it's gonna happen!

Lt. Herrera (*waving his hand in front of his face*): There's nothing up there!

Steven: There's even less now.

Major Linke: Turn back around and put your clothes back on.

Steven begins the long process of getting dressed.

Narrator: Having been caught a second time, I went to trial in September and was duly sentenced to forty-five years for the theft PLUS another twenty years for the July escape. An additional sixty-five years!

Well, that was just outrageous. So, that December, I escaped prison for a third time, this time dressed as a doctor.

I dyed a white pair of prison scrubs green in my cell toilet using Magic Marker pens, and I walked out the prison's front door for the third time. I met up with Phillip and the two of us fled to Mississippi.

But, ten days later, I had been caught again and was back behind bars.

Now, here's a bit of free advice for you. There are only so many times you can escape through a prison's front door before the warden and guards eventually catch on to what you're doing. Take it from me, three is about the limit.

Nevertheless, I was determined that nothing was going to keep Phillip and me apart. We were in love! So, my fourth escape was by far my most elaborate.

What it comes down to is this: the reason they caught me the three previous times was because the authorities realized I had escaped. For my fourth escape, I needed them to let me go. Then, when they went to my cell and saw that I wasn't there, they would say: "It doesn't matter. We let him go, remember?" Sounds crazy, right? Well, that's what I set out to make happen.

Despite my three prior escapes and all the stress I'd put my body through, I was still in surprisingly good health. In order for my plan to work, I needed to change that. So, I arranged for my prison medical records to be falsified to say that I'd tested HIV-positive. Then I lost a huge amount of weight in order to better fake the symptoms of late-stage AIDS.

My fictitious ill health was made all the more believable because AIDS was exactly what Jimmy had died from. I suppose they must have thought I got it from him. Anyway, fourteen months later in February 1998, believing I was about to die, the authorities released me from prison and admitted me to a hospice, near San Antonio, on special-needs parole.

On the outside I looked weak and emaciated. But on the inside I was very much alive and ready to make my next move. I called the hospice's manager on an internal phone, from not more than 50 feet away from where he was sitting, and pretended to be a doctor who specialized in experimental AIDS treatment. I told him I wanted a patient of his for my program. Then, a week or so after I had myself discharged to take part in the fictitious treatment, I declared myself dead. I even forged my own death certificate for good measure.

Steven is now handcuffed again, though not fully manacled as previously. The cubicle is taken apart by Major Linke while Lt. Herrera guards Steven.

Narrator: It was brilliant, even if I do say so myself. I was free and they thought I was dead. What could be more perfect? (*He gets a little angry*) What could go wrong, you must be wondering, because obviously something did to land me here in this X-rated freak show?

The Narrator exits stage right. Major Linke re-enters stage left. A light, illuminates Steven's new cell for the first time and the blue bar door next to them.

Major Linke (*to Lt. Herrera*): Take him to his cell.

Steven is taken through the blue bar door by Lt. Herrera. Major Linke exits stage left.

Lt. Herrera (*to someone offstage*): Roll 24.

The door of Steven's cell slides open and he is placed inside. The cell is otherwise empty.

Lt. Herrera: Close 24.

The cell door slides closed.

Lt. Herrera (*to Steven*): Come to the door.

Steven backs up to his cell door and Lt. Herrera removes his handcuffs through the cell's letterbox.

Major Linke walks onstage to give Steven a supply of basic rations. These are passed to him through the letterbox. The rations include powdered toothpaste, toilet paper, a bar of soap, a hand towel, some commissary forms and a pencil.

Major Linke (*to Steven*): Welcome home, Russell. We kept the lights on for you.

Steven (*slumping down on his bed*): Whatever.

ACT ONE

SCENE TWO

The Narrator enters stage right. A spotlight falls on him.

Narrator (*addressing the audience*): So, here's what went wrong.

Having been released from the hospice on March 13, I managed to live as a free, dead man until April 7. Twenty-six glorious days. It doesn't sound like much does it, when you consider it took 15 months of hard work to make happen? How did they catch me, when to all intents and purposes I was dead? Phillip, of course.

Steven is now sitting in his cell listening to the Narrator, though the Narrator doesn't realize.

Although I was a free man, Phillip remained incarcerated in TDCJ's Estelle Unit. I had to see him. Back then, he was pretty much my reason for living… and escaping. So, after renting and furnishing an apartment in Galveston, I telephoned Phillip, posing as his attorney.

Steven nods his head.

Narrator: The Estelle Unit had been Phillip's home ever since he'd been given twenty years for his part in the $800,000 NAMM embezzlement. But with me now officially dead and scant other evidence against him, I thought I could get him acquitted on appeal. Since attorney-to-inmate phone calls aren't recorded, I was able to tell him how I'd faked my own death, how much I loved him, and that we'd be together again soon. At the time, I meant every word.

After our call, I contacted a real attorney who wanted $50,000 to represent Phillip. Where the hell was I going to find that kind of money? It would take too long to earn legitimately and no one in their right mind would lend a sum like that to me.

So, when I applied to NationsBank for a $75,000 loan, $50,000 for Phillip and $25,000 for sundry expenses, I decided to use the name of an old acquaintance of mine: Art Sandler.

Steven mouths the name 'Art Sandler'.

Narrator: He at least was alive. I was officially dead.

Well, that's where things started to go wrong. Evidently the bank-teller must have gotten suspicious because, after not too long, I was whisked off into an office by two security guards, who confiscated my fake ID and called the F.B.I.

As you can imagine, I wasn't quite ready to return to jail, so I did what any decent, law-abiding citizen would do: I faked a heart attack.

Steven laughs to himself.

Narrator: An hour later, I was in a private room at the Baylor Medical Center E.R. department. Unfortunately, I hadn't counted on the two police officers who were stationed outside, waiting for me to feel better.

Happily though, they hadn't confiscated my cell phone, so I was able to call the local police station, misidentify myself as 'Special Agent Thomas of the F.B.I.' and instruct them they were no longer required to detain their suspect. They left the hospital and shortly afterwards so did I!

It had been a close call though. So close, that I decided to go and see Phillip in person to tell him all about it.

Now, in order to keep up the pretense that I was Phillip's lawyer, I needed a state bar I.D. card. I managed to obtain one, using the name of a real attorney, but that must have set off some internal alarm bells, because the bar office decided to circulate my picture among various Texan law-enforcement agencies.

Steven listens to details he is hearing for the first time.

Narrator: Now, it just so happened that one of the officers who saw that picture was a TDCJ official by the name of Terry Cobbs.

Cobbs knew my face well. He'd been part of the team that caught me in Biloxi after my third escape. After some digging, he found out that I'd been released on special parole and decided to call the hospice I'd been sent to. They, of course, told him I was dead. He, of course, didn't believe it.

He tracked Phillip down to the Estelle Unit, whereupon he was told that an attorney had recently paid him a visit. Cobbs must have guessed it was me because he and some local deputies laid a trap to snare me if I ever returned.

But I didn't. Visiting Phillip was a big risk and one that I wasn't planning on taking again any time soon. I also knew it would be easier to raise the money for a real attorney out of state. So that was where I headed.

Steven nods in agreement.

Narrator: So, while they were waiting for me at the Estelle Unit, I was driving from Livingston, Texas, to Fort Lauderdale, Florida. I also figured it didn't hurt to put a few states between me and Texas. I called Phillip along the way to let him know the progress I was making.

Once in Florida, I decided the only way I could raise $50,000 would be to repeat an old trick of mine. See, back when Jimmy had been diagnosed with AIDS, I'd gone out and bought a series of life insurance policies for him, which I then sold on to various viatical companies.

In return for paying me more than the cash value of each policy, they got to claim the full amount from the life insurance company when Jimmy died. It's sort of like when people reverse-mortgage their homes. Obviously, I never told the insurance companies that Jimmy had AIDS, otherwise they wouldn't have insured him. Typically I waited a few months before surprising them with the diagnosis.

Jimmy may have long since passed away, but I knew another person with AIDS whom I might be able to cash in on: ME! I didn't actually have AIDS, but I had a shitload of documentation that said I did. So, I thought, why not? Then, to make matters even easier, I decided I wouldn't even bother with real insurance policies. I'd just forge them on my computer.

After I'd printed out a couple, I called up a few local viatical companies. But unfortunately so did Terry Cobbs. He knew my background in insurance fraud and had somehow tracked me down to Florida. I suppose it must have been the calls I made to Phillip.

Steven stands up from his bunk and interrupts.

Steven (*loudly*): So there I was, last week in Sunrise, Florida. I'd just had dinner and decided to head out and get some antibiotics, just in case I'd need them after the plastic surgery. I left my rented apartment, walked over to my car... and some bastard put a gun to my head and told me I was under arrest!

Narrator (*to Steven for the first time*): That was Cobbs!

Steven: Was it? Well, who the fuck are you then and how do you know so much about my business?

Narrator (*laughing*): Haven't you been listening? I'm you!

Steven: You're me?

Narrator: That's right.

Steven: So, I'm talking to myself, right now?

Narrator: In a manner of speaking, yes.

Steven: Then that's it! (*He throws himself back on his bunk*) I've finally gone mad.

Narrator: Oh, you're not mad.

Steven (*sitting up*): No? Well then maybe they inserted some kind of anal probe in me just now when I wasn't looking.

Narrator: They didn't, I was watching.

Steven: Oh, you were, were you?

Narrator: Plus, I think you would have felt it if they had.

Steven: You want to know what I think? I think, if I fall asleep, you won't be here when I wake up.

Narrator: Well, there's gratitude for you! You should be grateful I'm here. You're going to need some company in the years to come. You mark my words.

Steven (*defiantly*): I don't need anyone.

Narrator: Well, good. Because I'm not anyone. I'm you.

Steven notices the Narrator is standing outside of his cell.

Steven (*puzzled*): How did you get out there?

Narrator: Out where?

Steven: Out there, How come I'm in here, but you're out there?

Narrator: Is it upsetting you?

Steven: No, I just want to know.

Narrator: Well I suppose it's because I'm not subject to the same limitations as you.

Steven: You mean you're not real.

Narrator: I'm real to you… And I can be anywhere you want me to be.

Steven: Anywhere?

Narrator: Anywhere.

Steven: Then fuck off and leave me alone.

Narrator (*laughing*): Well, I can be anywhere but that.

Steven: Figures.

Narrator: I don't make the rules.

Steven: Then who did, because it sure as hell wasn't me.

Narrator: The fact is: I'm staying.

Steven: Oh, we'll see about that.

Narrator: What?

Steven (*closing his eyes*): I'm going to count to five and when I open my eyes you're not going to be here.

Narrator: OK.

Steven (*calmly with his eyes closed*): 1-2-3-4...

The Narrator walks into Steven's cell and stands above him.

Steven: ...5

Narrator: Boo!

Steven jumps up from his bunk.

Steven: Jesus Christ! Get the fuck away from me.

Narrator: Am I gone?

Steven: No.

Narrator: And why would you want me gone? Don't you like your own company?

Steven: If you're me, what's my favorite color?

Narrator: Really? I just spilled every detail of your life on the run for the past 26 days and you want to test me by asking what our favorite color is?

Steven: You could be an undercover cop!

Narrator: One that walks through walls? (*Sarcastically*) They have lots of those, don't they?

Steven (*insisting*): What is my favorite color?

Narrator (*angrily*): You don't have a favorite color. Favorite colors are for teenage girls.

Steven: What am I about to say?

Narrator: When?

Steven: Now.

Both: Mary had a little... (*They pause*)... Bear.

Steven: Damn it!

Narrator: You see?

Steven: You're really me?

Narrator: Don't you recognize beauty when you see it?

Steven: No, I remember why I was contemplating plastic surgery.

Narrator: Look, quit playing around and start filling in one of those commissary order forms. The food in here sucks and we both know you're starving. If we're lucky we can catch the last round of the day.

Steven: You think?

Narrator: You're hungry, right?

Steven: I could eat a horse right now.

Narrator: I'm not sure that's on the list.

Steven grabs a commissary form and the pencil and sits on the floor of his cell, leaning against his bunk, scribbling. The Narrator comes over and sits on the bunk beside him.

Steven: Fifteen months I starved myself for. Fifteen fucking months!

Narrator: Be grateful, you'd have to pay a fat-farm a fortune for results like that. Ooh, you know what would taste good right now?

Steven: What?

Narrator: Chocolate.

Steven (*agreeing*): Yeah!

Narrator (*peering over Steven's shoulder*): Oh, get Butterfingers.

Steven (*marking the form*): Good call!

Narrator: And Milky Ways.

Steven: Yep.

Narrator: M&Ms?

Steven: Peanut M&Ms!

Narrator: And get a Snickers too.

Steven: Oh, my God. Right now, I would kill for a Snickers bar!

Narrator: We're on death row, honey. One of your neighbors probably did.

Steven: What else?

The Narrator gets out a nail file and begins filing his nails.

Narrator: Chicken noodles?

Steven: Chicken and beef noodles!

Narrator: Oh, and we need coffee and milk

Steven writes it down.

Steven: Got it.

The Narrator puts his feet up on the bunk.

Narrator: And tea. Oh, and I fancy oatmeal for breakfast.

Steven: Oatmeal. Check.

Narrator: And orange juice, but not the kind with…

Both: All the bits in it…

Narrator: And get some grapefruit juice as well.

Steven: Yep.

Narrator (*peering over Steven's shoulder*): And some Frosted Mini Wheats.

Steven: Mini Wheats…

Narrator: And I think some pastries would be nice.

Steven: What about ice cream?

Narrator: Ooh… Half a dozen Fudge Bombsticks and some Rainbow Freezes. You'd better get some Colgate too, because I am not using that powdered shit they've given us. Oh, and we need dental floss.

Steven: What about meat? Tuna?

Narrator: Fuck that shit, I need sugar!

Steven: And what would sir like to drink?

Narrator: I think some Coca Cola, Dr. Pepper, Grape Soda, Lemon Lime, Red Flash Soda and Root Beer should do the trick.

Steven (*shaking his head*): Someone's thirsty!

Narrator: You're starving! You need to put on some fat for winter!

Steven: True.

Narrator: Now how much does all that come to?

Steven: Let's see…

Narrator: You always were good at math.

Steven (*disappointedly*): $106.70

Narrator: Oh. How much are we allowed?

Steven: You know perfectly well we can only spend seventy bucks at the commissary each week.

Narrator: How much would we save if we didn't get the toothpaste or dental floss?

Steven: $1.85

Narrator (*still filing his nails*): Oh, well. It doesn't really matter. The new Warden's frozen your prison account anyway.

Steven: He's… (*The penny drops*) He's done what?

Narrator: Frozen your prison account. Because you just escaped and had to be dragged back here all the way from Florida. You can't spend a dime.

Steven: Then why are we filling in commissary slips?

Narrator: Because sometimes I find thinking about food just as satisfying as actually eating it. I feel positively stuffed.

Steven (*angrily*): Well, I don't!

Steven throws the pencil and forms across the room.

Steven (*angrily*): Can you go away now? Please?

Narrator: I can't. It's just you and me now. Just the two of us…

Steven: The two of us, eh? What about Phillip?

Narrator: What about Phillip?

Steven: He's my boyfriend.

Narrator (*mimicking him*): He's my boyfriend.

Steven: He's the reason we're in this mess.

Narrator: Exactly!

Steven: You know I'd do it all again for him in a heartbeat.

Narrator: Well, that's the difference between you and me then.

Steven: I would never say such a thing.

Narrator: You would. And one day you will.

Steven: Who are you because you sure as hell aren't me?

Narrator: Maybe I'm your subconscious. Or maybe I'm the Ghost of Christmas Future just like in…

Steven: Dickens.

Narrator: Exactly! Maybe I'm the attorney you pretended to be, or the CFO you said you were. Maybe I'm the mask you've been wearing all these years or, who knows, maybe I'm the man beneath the mask.

Steven: You're nothing but a drama queen. Wait, how do you know there's a new Warden? We've never been in this joint before.

Narrator: I know because you know. Deep down or something. Maybe you saw his name on a bulletin board or a plaque on the way in. The fact of the matter is there is a new Warden. I'm sure you'll have the pleasure of meeting him tomorrow.

Steven: If this is really happening, how am I not mad?

Narrator: You're just stressed. You've just been thrown back in the same place you spent fifteen months trying to leave. What makes my blood boil though, is not that you don't believe who I say I am, but that you fail to see that it's your misplaced obsession with Phillip that got you caught again.

Steven: I always get caught. That's the way life seems to turn out.

Narrator: They thought you were dead! You could be laying on a beach in Mexico right now. Or laying low in a city like Seattle or New York.

Steven: Doing what?

Narrator: Who the fuck knows! Picking fruit or something.

Steven: In New York City?

Narrator: Driving a cab then. The point is they caught you like they always catch you. Because they knew exactly where Phillip was and they knew he'd lead them straight to you. He's like an albatross around your neck.

Steven: He is not an albatross!

Narrator: My mistake. He's more nelly than that. More like a flamingo.

Steven: Puh.

Narrator: You know you bent over backwards to keep him out of prison for the NAMM job.

Steven: He's a good guy!

Narrator: He's a leach. A parasite! You know he was as guilty as you were, but you still tried to spare him a jail sentence. He was guiltier when you think about it, because at least you had the guts and the brains to pull it off. He never would have. You should have cut the cord.

Steven: So, if you're some kind of future me, tell me why I didn't!

Narrator (*reluctantly*): Because you're a creature of passion. Of obsession. Deep down in your heart you still love him because you need to be loved and because you think he loves you too.

Steven: He does love me.

Narrator: Have you heard the expression 'If you love somebody set them free'?

Steven: Yes.

Narrator: Well, there's another saying and it goes: 'If someone keeps getting you thrown in prison, you need to fucking move on!'

Steven: I'm supposed to take care of him.

Narrator: That's what he wants you to think. He's not stupid.

Steven: What does that mean?

Narrator: He used you.

Steven: When you overanalyze emotions and feelings, you can argue that everyone uses everybody else.

Narrator: Well, that's cheery.

Steven (*pause*): Do I ever make it out of here?

Narrator: Do you really want to know?

Steven: I think so.

Narrator: Well, let's see. You've escaped prison four times, so far. You're certainly capable of escaping again, but, let's face it, after that last escapade you're going to be kept under very close watch. It might be impossible to escape again.

Steven: Nothing is impossible.

Narrator: There is another option…

Steven: Which is?

Narrator: That they release you one day on parole.

Steven (*dismissively*): That's never going to happen.

Narrator: You're still eligible for parole, even now. You know that. You may have made fools of them, but not once during any of your crimes did you carry a gun, raise a hand or use force. Too much respect for those in law enforcement, I suspect. The ex-policeman in you, no doubt.

Steven: Wouldn't parole take years of good behavior?

Narrator: More than you can imagine.

Steven: I don't know if I could do that.

Narrator: Well, we'll find out together.

Steven: Will we? How long are you going to be around?

Narrator: I don't know. I dare say I'll be here for as long as you need me.

Steven: Do you snore?

Narrator: Just as badly as you do.

Steven: Well, you'll have to sleep on the floor, because you're sure as hell not sharing my bed.

Narrator: I wouldn't dream of it. First of all, you're not my type. And secondly, as you so brilliantly observed, I can go anywhere I want.

ACT ONE

SCENE THREE

The next day. Steven and the Narrator are snuggled up together on the cell's bed. Steven is lying closest to the audience. The Narrator wakes up first and caresses Steven's face.

Narrator: Good morning, handsome.

Steven (*still half asleep*): Phillip? Is that you?

Narrator: Did you sleep well?

Steven (*still with his eyes closed*): Kind of. I had the strangest dream.

Narrator: Really? What about?

Steven: I dreamt that someone called Cobbs captured me in Fort Lauderdale and took me back to prison.

Narrator: How silly. How would they have known where you were?

Steven: They recorded the calls I made to you in prison.

Narrator: Did they? So where are we now then?

Steven: In bed.

Narrator: Right. And where is that bed?

Steven: In the bedroom, dummy.

Narrator: Yes… and the bedroom is in the house and the house is in which town?

Steven: Biloxi? *(Confused)* Where do we live now?

Narrator *(coldly)*: The Gabriel Unit, Texas.

Steven *(jumping up)*: What????

Narrator: Home, sweet home.

Steven: You?!

Narrator: Were you expecting someone else?

Steven: But… I thought you were a figment of my imagination.

Narrator: I am.

Steven: Well, I thought you'd be gone when I woke up.

Narrator: You really are an ungrateful son-of-a-bitch.

Steven: But it's not normal to talk to yourself as much as this, let alone be able to look across the room and see yourself.

Narrator: You're not normal, Steven. Therefore, neither am I.

Steven: You were supposed to sleep on the floor.

Narrator: Well, I did for a while. But I can tell you one thing: your back doesn't get any better with age.

Steven: Why am I dressed?

Narrator: Because it's 11 a.m.

Steven: What?

Narrator: Major Linke delivered your breakfast at 3.30 a.m. You took one mouthful of the oatmeal and threw up in the toilet. Well, I say in the toilet... You managed to miss most of it. 'On' the toilet would be more apt.

Steven (*looking at the toilet*) Gross.

Narrator: Then you showered at 5.30 a.m. Slept for a bit. You had lunch at 9.30 a.m., which though not up to Marriott, Hilton or even Denny's standards was at least more palatable than breakfast. Then you fell asleep again.

Steven: Do you know what was wonderful about those twenty-six days of freedom I just had?

Narrator: The constant fear that you were going to get caught?

Steven: Being able to get up when the sun rises. Sunlight, unobscured by walls and windows. Air conditioning. Traffic. People going to work. Supermarkets...

Narrator: Old people with leathery skin, playing bridge and slowly decomposing...

Steven: Eh?

Narrator: You were in Florida, weren't you?

Steven: I need to get myself a new radio.

Narrator: What happened to the old one?

Steven: I left it at the hospice.

Narrator: Why on earth did you do that?

Steven: Because I was meant to be dying! I didn't think taking all of my belongings with me sent the right message. I wasn't supposed to have any use for them, was I?

Narrator: You could have told them you wanted to be buried with it! Anyway, look sharp, you're due to meet the warden any moment.

Steven: I am? How do you know that?

Narrator: Just a hunch.

Major Linke (*from outside the cell*): Come to the door!

Narrator: It's like I'm psychic.

Steven: Psychotic, more like.

Steven walks over to the cell door, turns around and has his hands cuffed through the letterbox. Once cuffed he moves away again.

Major Linke: Roll 24!

Steven's cell door slides open

Major Linke: Come on.

Steven (*to the Narrator, as he disappears though the door*): So what's he going to say to me?

Narrator: The usual: meal times, health and safety regulations, and what time the pool opens and closes. That kind of thing.

Steven: Aren't you coming?

Narrator (*standing*): Of course I am. (*He points downstage to the warden's office*) But I think I'll take the short cut.

Steven is brought round the back of his cell, and the stage, to Warden Alvarado's office. The narrator doesn't go this way. He walks across the stage from Steven's cell to stand in the warden's office. This is his 'short cut'.

Major Linke knocks on the door of the warden's office.

Warden: Enter.

Major Linke and Steven enter. The Warden is sitting at his desk wearing a dark suit. Steven is made to sit in a seat opposite the Warden.

Major Linke: Inmate number 0760259, as ordered, sir.

Warden (*leaning forward and reading off a piece of paper on his desk*): Steven. J. Russell.

Narrator: The sign on the door says Warden Alvarado.

Warden (*looking up at Steven*): Did you have a nice vacation?

Steven: I did, thank you. Although I'd planned on being away for longer.

Warden: I'm sure you did. Well, I'm sorry to have to tell you this, Russell, but that's the last little trip you'll be taking for a while. From here on in I'm going to have you so far behind bars, you'll have to get your sunshine shipped in by UPS.

Steven: I'm pretty sure my last warden said something similar.

Warden: Did he now? Well, you're my prisoner now and you're going to play by my rules.

Steven: He said that too. Do they give you guys a script or something? In warden school or wherever it is you go to become the boss of a place like this?

Warden: Keeping scum, like you, behind bars has been in my family for generations. My daddy was a warden and his daddy before him. I've seen thousands like you come and go.

Steven: Did it occur to you to rebel and maybe run a restaurant or a hotel instead?

Warden: You're funny, Russell, but know this: I always get the last laugh. In the fifteen years I've been Warden, no one has ever escaped from one of my prisons.

Steven: Well now, that just sounds like a dare.

Warden: Do it! I'll have you shot before you reach the perimeter fence. You may be able to walk through walls, but I don't think you can dodge bullets. I run the tightest jails in Texas and there's no way on God's Earth that you are going to make a fool out of me.

Narrator (*to Steven*): Dallas County Jail.

Steven (*turning to the Narrator*): What?

Narrator: October 1995.

Steven (*to the Narrator*): Oh my God, you're right.

Warden: Who's right? Russell, who are you talking to?

Steven: We've met before, Warden.

Warden: I don't think so.

Steven: Oh, we have. I remember it vividly.

Warden: Were you in one of my previous prisons?

Steven: In a way, yes. I met you in October, 1995, while visiting one of your inmates, Phillip Morris. My boyfriend. I pretended to be Phillip's attorney, something I did again quite recently. Your guards fell for it hook, line and sinker.

Warden: Did they now?

Steven: You don't remember? You and I had a meeting afterwards in your office. You had Phillip working field squad, digging up weeds, and I told you the pollen was playing havoc with his allergies. You very kindly had him transferred to janitorial services.

Warden (*coldly*): What?

Steven: Of course, he doesn't actually have any allergies. I just had you transfer him to make his life a little bit easier. He sure was mighty grateful.

The Narrator starts laughing.

Warden (*shouting*): Who the fuck do you think you are?

Steven: Please don't shout, Warden. I have very sensitive ears.

Warden: I don't give a fuck about your ears! (*Pointing*) I'm going to make sure you regret that stunt, you little prick!

Steven: Language, Warden, please. (*He points to Major Linke*) There are ladies present.

Warden (*enraged*): You think I don't have the power to make your life hell in here? You think I can't keep you here? You're not going anywhere! Nowhere, do you hear me? Not ever! Not while I'm Warden, not even after I'm Warden! You are probably going to die in this prison, Russell, and do you know why? Because you're scum! You're a screw-up! (*He calms, remembering something he thinks is clever*) Your mother didn't want you, did she? Gave you up for adoption, didn't she?

Steven: Does it say that in my file, Warden? You must read awful well.

Warden (*fuming*): Do you know why she got rid of you? Because she knew you were a fuck-up! She knew you were damaged goods, that's why.

Steven: You seem to know my biological mother very well. Are you my biological father?

Warden (*still enraged*): Everything you've touched has turned to shit, Russell. Everything. Your career in law-enforcement? Did you really think that was going to work out? It's not a career for faggots! Being a police officer requires integrity, being able to live with and tell the truth. Maybe if you hadn't been so busy trying to bum all your buddies while on duty, you would have realized that.

Steven: Did I mention I 'bummed' Phillip in your prison shortly before that meeting I had with you? I'm amazed you couldn't smell it on me. Did we shake hands?

Warden: You're a pervert, Russell.

Steven: Does it say that in my file, Warden? What else does it say?

Warden: It says that you're beyond redemption. There's no hope for you. You may be all over *The Prison Times*, but you're just a low-life criminal, you hear me? Not the celebrity you seem to think you are. You are never going to see your little muse of a boyfriend again. Never! Do you hear me? I'm going to see to that.

Steven: Do you suffer from constipation Warden, because you look like you could use some prune juice or something similar? (*He turns to Major Linke*) Would you be a darling and go get some for the Warden?

Warden: I don't know what kind of a country you think this is, but this isn't some liberal, lefty, handout society where you can just take what you want and give nothing back. This is America. And this is Texas! It's survival of the fittest here. It's pick-yourself-up-by-your-own-bootstraps. Where, if you work hard you get rewarded and if you fuck around with the system then you get fucked by the system! (*He points at Steven*) You hurt people, Russell. That $800,000 that you spent on earrings and chocolates for your fuck-buddy? That was someone's hard-earned cash. Hard, honest work the like of which you have never done.

Steven: Is that what this is about? Jealousy? Because I spent more money in four months than you'll earn in your entire career? What would you do with that kind of money, Warden? Have you thought about it?

Narrator (*to Steven*): He could buy himself a decent suit for starters.

The Warden bangs his fist on the table.

Warden: It's about the law, Russell. And about God. You're on the wrong side of both right now and, since you're incapable of realizing that, it's my job to make sure that you never get to harm another human being.

He calms down and takes a piece of paper out of his desk drawer.

That's why I've drawn up a special set of protocols for you. I thought I'd share them with you.

Steven: Special treatment? I never knew you cared.

Warden: Oh, I care, Russell. Which is why from now until the day you die you're going to be housed in the most secure part of this prison: death row.

Narrator: Tell us something we don't know.

Steven: At least I'll have some interesting neighbors to talk to.

Warden: Unlike your neighbors though, you will be moved to a different cell every 72 hours.

Steven: Well, they say a change is as good as a rest.

Warden: Your cell will subject to a daily search by two guards and a supervisor.

Steven: Good. It's about time they had some work to do.

Warden: You will only be allowed to recreate and shower in the same section as your cell. And every thirty minutes, day and night, you will be subject to observation by a guard to confirm you are present in your cell and in compliance with all prison rules and regulations. Any maintenance conducted on your cell will only be carried out in the presence of one of my guards.

Staff members will not converse with you except to give you orders. If, for any reason, you have to leave death row, two guards and a supervisor will accompany you. You will wear a shackle blast whenever you leave the building. All correspondence to and from you will be photocopied and read by the mailroom supervisor, an internal affairs investigator and a unit psychologist.

Steven: All of that sounds expensive. I hope I won't be too much of a drain on your resources, Warden.

Warden: I hope you don't like sleep or privacy too much.

Steven: And you think all that will work? Do you think that will keep me from escaping again if I set my mind to it?

Warden: If I didn't, I wouldn't be sharing the details with you, would I?

Steven: So, the real question, is what details aren't you sharing with me?

Warden: I've enjoyed our little chat, Russell. That will be all. (*He looks down at the paperwork on his desk*) Take the prisoner back to his cell.

Steven: Before I go, the guys wanted me to tell you what an honor it is to have you as our Warden.

Warden (*not looking up*): Did they now?

Steven: Speaking personally, I can honestly say that I have never met a cleverer man in my entire life. I mean, you must know everything about everything. It certainly is going to be a challenge breaking out of this joint.

Warden (*still looking down*): That's the idea.

Steven: But I promise that when I do, I'll send you a postcard and a gift basket from wherever it is I end up.

Warden (*to Major Linke, looking up*): Get him out of here.

Major Linke begins to walk Russell out of the Warden's office and back to his cell.

Steven: I'm thinking Puerto Rico. Or The Bahamas. (*From behind the scenery*) Actually, I hear Vancouver is lovely this time of year.

Major Linke: Roll 24!

Steven Russell steps back into his cell. The Narrator is waiting for him having taken his short cut across the stage.

Major Linke: Close 24!

Steven Russell's handcuffs are removed through the cell door's letterbox.

Narrator (*to Steven*): Well, you sure showed him.

Steven: What?

Narrator: Did you see his face when you mentioned seeing Phillip at the Estelle Unit?

Steven: He looked like he realized he had to shit out a basketball!

Narrator: He's probably squatting in his en-suite, right now, heaving and groaning.

Steven laughs a little and lies down on his bed.

Steven: Did you hear all of those rules he's implementing for us?

Narrator: I sure did.

Steven: How the hell am I going to get out of here with people watching me every thirty minutes?

Narrator: You really want to escape again?

Steven: More than ever. I want to show that arrogant little fuck what a useless prick he really is!

Narrator: Well, there are plenty of ways you can get at him without escaping.

Steven: How?

Narrator: You're already occupying space in his head. Just by reminding him about that meeting you had with him. Why don't we just try and occupy a little bit more of his head every day?

Steven: You mean just stay here and throw sand in the machinery? I know you're not real, but don't you miss the outside world? There must be someone you care for out there that you want to see, even if it's not Phillip.

Narrator: We've escaped from prison four times now, right?

Steven: Right.

Narrator: And how many actual days were we free?

Steven: I've never counted.

Narrator: Just over two years the first time, five days the second time, ten days the third time and twenty-six days the fourth.

Steven: Well, this time we won't get caught.

Narrator: We always get caught! No matter how brilliant the plan or how perfectly executed it is, Phillip always gets us caught! If we escape a fifth time, they're going to come looking for us. You'll make the FBI's Most Wanted list this time. They'll put up a reward to get you back behind bars. No one makes a fool of the Texas Department of Criminal Justice five times in a row and gets away with it.

Steven laughs.

Steven: Well, we'll go back down to Mexico or somewhere where they don't have an extradition process.

Narrator: This is America. Everyone has an extradition treaty with us. And we tried Mexico before, remember? We came back. Anyway it's not as easy to skip the country these days. The controls are getting tighter.

Steven: So, what are you saying?

Narrator: I'm saying we need to sit this one out.

Steven: You're serious?

Narrator: I've never been more serious.

Steven (*pointing towards the warden's office*): And let him talk to us like that?

Narrator: Hell, no!

Steven: Let him think that he owns us? That he's better than us just because his daddy and granddaddy put in good words for him down at the golf club?

Narrator: Of course not. The man is a piece of shit. (*Pause*) But it's time to realize two things. One: escaping prison, unlike most other crime, does not pay. It really doesn't. It's not getting us anywhere except further and further behind bars.

Steven: What's the second thing?

Narrator: You need to let go of Phillip. The warden's right on that one. You are never going to see him again.

Steven: He can't do that to us.

Narrator: He can. And he can't. Phillip's locked up right now, so it's not exactly a burning issue. We can deal with it when he gets out. Maybe you'll want to see him by then. But maybe you won't.

Steven: Of course I'll want to see him.

Narrator: But you're right about one thing.

Steven: What?

Narrator: No one talks to us like that and gets away with it.

Steven: So what are we going to do to rattle his cage if we're not going to escape?

Narrator: He's trying to drive you mad, Steven. That's what solitary confinement is all about. Hell, on the outside you'd be arrested for treating a dog the way they plan on treating you. We're going to fight it and we're going to turn the tables on him. Mess with his head and see how he likes it.

Steven: Structure and self-discipline, that's how you stop yourself from losing it.

Major Linke interrupts their conversation.

Major Linke (*from outside the cell door*): Mail call!

The letterbox to Steven's cell opens and a flurry of paper comes through and lands on the floor. Steven walks over and picks it all up and returns to his bunk.

Narrator *(he gets an idea)*: Literature! That's what we need. Newspapers, books and magazines. You should subscribe to the *Wall Street Journal, USA Today, The New York Times* and *Time Magazine*!

Steven *(flicking through the mail)*: Plus a handful of gay lifestyle magazines. Just to give those women from the rotary club, who read the mail here, something to think about.

Narrator: *The Advocate, OUT* and… *Details* should do it.

Steven: And I need to get another radio.

Narrator: You sure do. Don't worry about a clock. We'll be able to tell the time from the guards checking in on us. Every half hour, right? Anything interesting in the mail?

Steven: I don't know. Here, you open some.

Steven hands the Narrator some letters.

Narrator: We sure are popular.

Steven: Who's yours from?

Narrator: Ugh!? It's from one of the god-squad.

Steven: Already?

Narrator: They must think you're going to be executed because you're here on death row. Where did they get our name from? *(Reading)* "It is never too late to repent. I hope and pray you accept the Lord Jesus Christ into your heart as your Savior…"

Steven: They haven't thought that one through, have they? I mean, if I was about to be pumped full of pentobarbital, my heart isn't exactly the safest place to be.

Narrator (*still reading*): "Please take time to read the following bible verses." Their spelling is atrocious. They've spelled verses V-E-R-S-U-S. They should stop reading the Bible and start reading a dictionary. And their handwriting sucks. God has not been kind to them. Who's yours from?

Steven: A gay kid in Montana.

Narrator: Well that sounds altogether more promising.

Steven: Says he's sixteen years old. (*Reading*) "Dear Steven, My name is Arthur. I go to Mountain High School in Chinook. I'm gay, but I haven't told my parents yet. Since reading about your prison escape in the local paper I've been imagining you locked up in your cell when I masturb..."

What?!!!!

Narrator (*rushing over*): Oh my God, that's hot! Is there a photo?

Steven: Yeah.

They both look at the photo included with the letter.

Both (*recoiling*): Eww!

Narrator: Well, maybe he has an older, more handsome brother?

Steven: It's probably not even a picture of him.

Narrator: I can think of more attractive people he could pretend to be.

Steven: Some crusty eighty-year old who wants us to write dirty things to him probably sent it.

Narrator: Maybe he has an attractive son or grandson, then?

Steven: If you were young and gay, why would you live in Montana? It doesn't seem likely does it? You'd leave as soon as you could and move to San Francisco or Los Angeles.

Narrator: Maybe he doesn't want to be where all the pretty people are?

Steven: Really? Have you been to San Francisco?

The Narrator opens another letter.

Narrator: This is from some guy called Steve McVicker.

Steven: Why does that name sound familiar?

Narrator (*reading out loud*): "Dear Steven, I was waiting for you at Houston Intercontinental Airport when you flew back to Texas after your latest 'excursion'. We were only told at the last minute that you were being flown to another airport. You must have really upset someone high-up this time. Publicly, when your plane failed to land, they said there was a mix-up with your flight. But I'm sure they were just blowing smoke up our asses."

"I've reported on a couple of your previous escapes for *The Houston Journal*, but this time the TDCJ's Media Relations Department hasn't been particularly friendly or responsive to my latest request to interview you. I'd like to write a full-page piece on your most recent escape. I contacted a buddy of mine at *The Prison Times* and from the few details he told me it sounds like you outdid yourself this time."

"If you're interested I'll try and arrange a media visit with your new Warden. If that fails perhaps we could do an interview some other way?"

"Yours truly, Steve McVicker."

That's perfect!

Steven: In what way?

Narrator: It would drive Alvarado crazy if our story was in *The Houston Journal!*

Steven: Which is precisely why he won't allow it.

Narrator: How can he refuse? And if he does we can either mail the details to him or put him on your visitors' list under 'friends and family'. It's outside his control. It'll drive him nuts!

Steven: You think?

Narrator: Didn't you hear him going on about how you're not a celebrity? He thinks he's the rock star around here, but we're the one they want to splash across a full page of *The Houston Journal*. I bet everyone at his country club reads that paper.

Steven: Agreed. We need to buy some stationery from the commissary and write him back. Maybe we can set something up for next week?

Narrator (*shaking his head*): It'll take that long just to get a letter out of here. You heard what they're gonna do with all our incoming and outgoing mail.

Steven: Well, the week after then.

Narrator: However long it takes, we'll make it happen. We just need to be patient. Very, very patient.

ACT ONE

SCENE FOUR

The lights come on in Warden Alvarado's office. The Warden is sat at his desk talking to Gabriel Unit's Media Relations Officer. She is dressed smartly.

Warden (*exasperated*): I won't allow it!

Media Relations Officer: What grounds do we have to refuse?

Warden: Grounds? We don't need to give a reason. He made fools out of us! That's what grounds we have.

Media Relations Officer: That's not good enough, I'm afraid.

Warden (*eying her up and down*): Just whose side are you on?

Media Relations Officer: Warden, do you know how many journalists we made enemies of when Russell's plane was diverted from Houston Intercontinental Airport?

Warden: It wasn't diverted, my dear. We both know it was never going to Houston Intercontinental.

Media Relations Officer: Exactly! We lied to them. I lied to them. To the press.

Warden: You didn't lie to them. You were deliberately kept in the dark so that you wouldn't have to lie.

Media Relations Officer: It's the same thing to them. Now, you may not like it, but the best way to keep good relations with the press corps is to manage them. We give and we take. We have to give them what they want from time to time so that we can call in favors when we need to do damage control.

Warden: I think you've gone native.

Media Relations Officer: I have good relationships with a lot of journalists, and yes, I count a number of them as friends. That's my job. It's called being professional. Now, are you going to authorize this media visit or do I have to transfer to another prison?

Warden: Are you threatening me?

Media Relations Officer: I'm trying to do my job. And if you won't let me do it properly then what choice do I have?

Warden: What can we do to contain the situation?

Media Relations Officer: Well, why don't we arrange for this McVicker to speak to the arresting officer? Cobbs, wasn't it? In addition to Russell. We could also offer him fifteen minutes with you? Or if you don't want to speak with him in person, I'll happily draft a statement for you.

Warden: Do we know what kind of story he wants to write?

Media Relations Officer: He's a journalist for a Texan newspaper and the story is about a prison escape. He's not going to be sympathetic. His readership don't want to read anything that portrays Russell as a victim. McVicker has always written dispassionately about Russell in the past. I don't see any reason why this time will be any different.

He'll want to discuss the escape with Russell, which will make us look foolish. He'll want to hear about his time on the run. Then his capture, which will make us look a bit better. My understanding is Cobbs did some good police work. We should make sure McVicker is aware of it. Show him that the system worked and that's why Russell is back behind bars.

Warden: You are to make it clear to him that I was not Warden when the escape took place, is that understood?

Media Relations Officer: I can do that.

Warden: Can we imply that I was brought in to ensure it doesn't happen again?

Media Relations Officer: My understanding is that wasn't the case. But if you want to spin it that way when you meet with him, I can't stop you.

Warden: I don't want to talk to him. Spin it for me. Draw up a statement and I'll sign off on it before you give it to him.

Media Relations Officer: I'll write it this afternoon.

The Media Relations Officer stands up from her chair, as if to leave.

Warden: And I want an embargo on whatever edition it ends up in. That story is not to make it inside the walls of this facility.

Media Relations Officer: You'll need to speak to Human Resources and the mailroom about that.

Warden: I'm speaking to you. See that it's done.

Media Relations Officer: Yes, warden.

Warden: That will be all.

The Media Relations Officer goes to leave again, but pauses.

Media Relations Officer: Warden?

Warden: Yes?

Media Relations Officer: I don't want this to affect our professional relationship. We have to let them interview Russell this time, but going forward I'm happy to work with you to make sure it doesn't become a regular occurrence.

Warden: I appreciate that.

Media Relations Officer: I can also set up a profile piece for you, if you like? 'The New Warden of Gabriel Unit.' In one of the local papers?

Warden: Now you're just sucking up.

She takes his comment as a 'no' and goes to leave.

Warden: Have a proposal on my desk first thing next week.

Media Relations Officer (*smiling*): Yes, sir.

ACT ONE

SCENE FIVE

The lights go on in the visitors' area where Steven is meeting Houston Journal reporter Steve McVicker. Steven is on one side of the Plexiglas, while McVicker sits on the other. The Narrator circles the two of them.

Steven: … then at 5 a.m. on what must have been April 17, I was transported from Broward County Jail in Fort Lauderdale, Florida, back to Texas by TDCJ fugitive apprehension officers Terry Cobbs, John Moriarity, Richard Dees and Paul Hunter…

McVicker: Moriarty, like in *Sherlock Holmes*?

Steven: Different spelling: M-O-R-I-A-R-I-T-Y.

McVicker: Got it. Is the fictional Moriarty a hero of yours?

Narrator: What kind of a question is that?

Steven (*to McVicker*): Oh, he's an amateur compared to me.

McVicker: At least he managed to stay out of prison.

Steven: So he could fall down some waterfall to his death! That doesn't sound too smart to me.

McVicker: You prefer where you are?

Steven: Compared to death? I think life is a heck of a lot better than the alternative.

McVicker: Even life in prison?

Steven: If it comes to that, yes.

McVicker: I take it you're not religious?

Narrator: We've given it up for Lent.

Steven: I might be soon, if the new warden has his way. He wants me to accept Jesus as my personal savior. There's certainly a vacancy in that department at the moment.

McVicker: I'm sorry. I interrupted you…

Steven: Right… then I was flown back to Texas, courtesy of the state's twin-engine Beechcraft and landed at a private airport adjacent to the Gurney Unit, Intake and Reception Transport Facility at Tennessee Colony.

McVicker: How was the flight?

Steven: The in-flight service left a lot to be desired. There was no movie and no salted peanuts. When it comes to private jets, I'm more of a Bombardier fan myself, but I understand that the state's budget is finite.

When we landed at Tennessee Colony, I was turned over to the custody of two wardens, two majors and eight additional guards, split across two transport vans and two cars.

McVicker: That's… twelve people?!

Steven: It felt like a presidential convoy. You have to understand,

Steve, I'm a huge threat to society and must be contained at any cost. Had I escaped again, goodness knows what might have happened. I might have gone shopping, read a newspaper or gotten a manicure or something. And that can never be allowed to happen. The security of Texas depends upon my incarceration, I'm sure you can see that.

McVicker: How much do you think it cost to bring you back into custody?

Steven: Isn't that for you to find out?

McVicker: Didn't you used to be a cop? Can you even guess what it would have cost?

Steven: You can always ask Warden Alvarado, although I'm sure he'll lowball you. The truth is it probably cost them less while I was on the run, even if you include all those expenses bringing me back here, than it costs to keep me here. Prison is very expensive, Steve. Death row especially. Now that the warden has all these new rules for the staff here, it must be costing them a small fortune.

McVicker: You can understand why he's determined to keep a close eye on you, right?

Steven: Oh, it's understandable. He told me the other day he's never had someone escape from one of his prisons before. He's an escapee virgin, if you will. Well, I'm not one for bragging, Steve, but I can't wait to pop that man's cherry.

McVicker: You'd consider escaping again?

Steven: What have I got to lose?

McVicker: Won't they be expecting it?

Steven: Initially, yes. But you're forgetting one thing. It's human nature to let your guard down after a while. Warden Alvarado may consider it his personal mission in life to keep me under lock and key, but the people that work here don't give a shit.

They're paid minimum wage and on a daily basis they have to deal with some of the biggest, craziest assholes in Texas. If that were your job, you'd cut corners as well, just to make your day a little easier. And then you'd end up making mistakes too. They're only human. Or as close to it as you can get. Plus TDCJ is cheap.

McVicker: In what way are they cheap?

Steven: The people of Texas do themselves a great disservice. They want to punish those of us who have erred, but they want to do it at next to no cost. I mean, why should they pay to keep us fed, housed and watered when there are children going hungry and old people without heating in the winter? That's their logic.

So, they allocate the minimal funds necessary and get inmates to do jobs that should be done by paid, law-abiding professionals. I'm talking administration, janitorial work, gardening, food delivery, cooking, and garbage collection. Those kind of things.

Now, if you were going to employ someone to work inside a prison, would you give the job to someone with a criminal record? Of course you wouldn't. But that's exactly what you're doing when you use prison labor. They do it because it's cheap. What's the flipside? They facilitate a black market in contraband that includes drugs, pornography, cell phones, inmate-to-inmate correspondence and weapons.

Until prisons are properly staffed, and those staff are properly paid, there will always be loopholes and cracks for people like me to squeeze through. Sufficient funds will never be provided to detain a state's or a country's wrongdoers, so there will always be escapes and escapees. It's a problem as old as time.

McVicker: That's very interesting. What would you do, if you were in the Warden's shoes, to keep you here?

Steven: Well, let me tell you…

McVicker and Steven Russell are plunged into half-light as the lights come on in Warden Alvarado's office. The Warden is speaking to Major Linke and Lt. Herrera.

Warden (*reading from a crumpled edition of The Houston Journal*): "At this point Russell leans forward in his chair, 'I'd be happy to share that information with him,' he says, 'for a price: my freedom and a regular pay check, say. It seems to me that there's no one better qualified than me to point out all the flaws in the system. But do you think he'd listen to me? He's so paranoid and dumb with fear that he probably wouldn't believe me anyway. But that's exactly what he should be doing if he wants to maintain his record of never having one of his prisoners escape.'" (*He throws the newspaper down on his desk and shouts.*) And where did you say you found this?

Lt. Herrera: In Russell's cell, sir.

Warden: And how did a newspaper, which I have personally banned from this facility, end up in Russell's cell?

Lt. Herrera: We don't know, sir.

Warden: You don't know?

Major Linke: Actually, I have an idea, sir.

Lt. Herrera looks sideways at Major Linke.

Warden: Do you Major? Would you care to share that insight with the rest of us?

Major Linke: There's a name and address on the front page, sir. An address label. The original owner of the newspaper must be a subscriber to *The Houston Journal*, sir.

Warden (*unfolding the newspaper*): There's a name? ... (*Reading out loud*) Warden Alvarado. This is my goddamned newspaper!

Major Linke: Yes, sir. I believe that explains how the newspaper got inside the prison, sir. It was delivered to you.

Warden: Don't play smart with me Major or I'll hang you by your balls in the recreation yard! I get this delivered every day and at the end of the day, once I'm finished with it, it goes in the…. (*He points to his office trash can with the paper in his hand. He pauses*) He's been going through my fucking trash!

Lt. Herrera: Sir, that's impossible. Russell cannot leave his cell unsupervised and has certainly not been in this part of the building.

Warden: Well, someone has! Lieutenant, I want you to interview every inmate on trash collection and find out who has been passing the contents of my trash can to Steven Russell. I want you to do this today and I want whoever it is off trash collection permanently. If another piece of my trash ends up in Russell's cell then the two of you will be collecting my trash personally, every day, until the day I die or retire. Is that clear?

Major Linke: Yes, sir!

The Warden throws the newspaper into the trash can.

Warden: Is nothing sacred around here?

ACT ONE

SCENE SIX

A spotlight shines on Steven's cell. Steven is on his bed, hiding a letter from the Narrator, who is trying to take it from him.

Narrator: Let me see it!

Steven: No.

Narrator (*he manages to grab hold of the letter but Steven doesn't let go*): He's my boyfriend too!

Steven: He is not. You don't even like him!

Narrator: Neither will you, eventually. Give it here!

Steven (*straining*): Fuck off!

Narrator (*still trying to pull it away*): Just let me read it!

Steven: Why? You'll just ridicule it.

Narrator: That depends on what it says.

Steven: You're going to rip it!

Narrator: Then give it to me and… it won't get… ripped. (*He manages pull the letter away*) Aha!

The Narrator runs to the other side of the cell. Steven stays on his bed.

Steven: Asshole.

Narrator (*reading in a sugar sweet voice*): "Dear Phillip…"

Steven: If you insist on reading it out aloud, at least do so in a normal voice. I already know what it says anyway, so the only reason you're doing this is to wind me up.

Narrator (*continuing in his normal voice*): "I guess by now you'll have heard the news that I'm back in prison. They caught up with me at the apartment in Fort Lauderdale. Don't blame yourself. I don't think it was the phone calls to you that helped them track me down. I always drove forty miles from the apartment every day, to call you from a payphone."

"Though they probably ended up recording our conversations when they realized I wasn't really your attorney, I don't think I ever said exactly where I was. Nevertheless, to say I'm pissed at being back in jail is an understatement. But you'll be pleased to know I'm channeling all my energy into undermining the new warden we have here. He's an arrogant idiot who thinks he's God's gift to law enforcement. He is most definitely not. Quite the opposite, in fact."

"All my ingoing and outgoing mail is being read and photocopied now so it's fair to assume he'll be reading this at some point. What follows is for his benefit as well as yours: Warden Alvarado is a jumped up redneck who was only given the job of warden because his daddy's friends gave it to him. I've only met with him once here, but just from that one encounter I could tell he's a short-dicked inbred with a wife who hasn't been fucked properly since she gave birth to their last child. She probably can't even spell orgasm, let alone remember what one actually feels like. I take that back. She might. I hear she's fucking everyone at their golf club behind his back."

Nice.

Steven: Thanks.

Narrator (*continuing reading*): "I thought I might have heard from you by now. I hope everything's OK between us and you got the flowers I sent you. I had to pull quite a few favors to get them delivered to you."

"I'm not blaming you, but I wish you'd gone with either my Plan A or Plan B for getting you out of jail. We could have been lying on a beach in Key West by now. I know you wanted to do things properly, but the truth is it would always have taken too long to go that route."

"As it turned out, I ended up getting caught trying to do things your way. They apprehended me while I was trying to raise the money to get you a decent appeal lawyer. Raising the money now that I'm back in jail is going to be much harder, although I have a few ideas if you'd like to hear them. Perhaps you'll get back to me on that."

"So, I have good news and bad news. The good news is, maybe because they don't want a trial or because they just want to keep it quiet, they're not charging me with my latest escape. The bad news is they've reconsidered their decision not to charge me with the 1996 Estelle Unit escape; my third. If you remember, the only reason they didn't charge me was because they thought I was dying of AIDS. Well, now they know I'm alive and well, and likely to remain that way, they've decided to press charges. The D.A. has offered me 30 years. It's all academic at this point."

"Anyway, I still love you and I can't wait to see you again. I don't know when that will be, but I'm hoping it will be soon. Love Steven."

Steven: Are you happy now?

Narrator: Happier than you, it turns out. You know there's a reason he hasn't written to you.

Steven: Is there? Other than the fact he has no idea where I am?

Narrator: He knows where you are. Everyone in the state knows where you are. The truth is he's just not interested any more.

Steven: That is not true.

Narrator: Open your eyes. He needs a boyfriend, not a pen pal.

Steven: He needs protecting.

Narrator: Well, a lot of good you're going to be able to do for him in here.

Steven: There's a lot I can do for him in here, actually.

Narrator: Well, good luck with that!

Steven: What I have in mind has nothing to do with luck.

Narrator: Well, then it hasn't got a snowball's chance in hell of working.

Blackout in Steven's cell.

The lights go on in Warden Alvarado's office. The Warden is sitting at his desk. Next to him sits Major Linke. Lt. Herrera brings a prisoner into the Warden's office. The prisoner is handcuffed behind his back.

Lt. Herrera: Prisoner 794033, sir.

Warden: Thank you. (*He looks down at the paperwork in front of him*) What do we have here?

Major Linke (*also looking down at paperwork*): Accessory to fraud. Some other minor convictions.

Prisoner (*politely*): I'm in the middle of an appeal. Um… I'm actually

71

innocent. There's been what you might call a misunderstanding.

Warden: There always is, Mr (*he rechecks the paperwork in front of him*) Morris. (*Sarcastically*) Everyone here is innocent. The state of Texas prides itself on incarcerating innocent men. Your prior conviction for theft-of-service suggests you're not exactly Snow White, however. Since you're no stranger to prison I'm sure you know what the purpose of this meeting is?

Prisoner: Work assignment?

Warden: That's right. As I'm sure you know by now, you're one of sixty homosexuals that have been transferred here from Estelle Unit. Had we known you were coming we'd obviously have rolled out the pink welcome mat, but since we didn't know you were coming until this morning, that wasn't possible.

Prisoner: Oh, my.

Warden (*firmly*): Let me be clear, Mr Morris. You've been moved here for your own safety, not because anyone here likes what it is that you do.

Major Linke (*to the Warden*): Custody level? G2. Minimum in?

Warden: Agreed.

Major Linke: Housing assignment: 7 building?

Warden: Yes.

Major Linke: Job assignment? He was a clerk at Estelle.

Warden (*to Major Linke*): Have we placed anyone in administrative segregation to work for Major Young?

Major Linke: No, sir.

Warden (*looking at the Prisoner but still talking to Major Linke*): He doesn't seem too smart, but he's quiet enough not to make trouble. (*To the Prisoner*) I'm assigning you to administrative segregation to work for Major Young. You will be his clerk. Do you understand?

Prisoner: Not entirely, no.

Warden: You know what administrative segregation is right?

Prisoner: Death row?

Warden: Close enough. Only those on ad seg, as we call it, are the ones they won't let us fry. You'll be doing paperwork for the Major. He's got a short fuse and won't stand for any Southern prissiness, do you understand? You'd do best to say as little as possible. Speak only when spoken to. Do that and you'll be fine.

At this point Major Linke begins to look anxious. He quickly passes a sheet of paper to the warden.

Warden (*oblivious*): You'll be housed with all the other queers, but know this: no funny business goes on in any of my prisons. Do you hear me? And if you are the subject of any sexual advances you are to notify a guard or the prison authorities immediately. We treat such instances very seriously, as the law requires us to.

Major Linke: Warden!

Warden (*still to the Prisoner*): I therefore hope this is the only time the two of us meet. (*He motions to Lt. Herrera*) That will be all.

Major Linke: Sir. That will not be all!

Warden: I beg your pardon?

Major Linke: With respect, sir, we're not done with the prisoner.

Warden: Why on Earth aren't we?

Major Linke: Sir, look at his name!

The Warden looks down at the piece of paper Major Linke places in front of him. He is none the wiser.

Warden: P. C. Morris.

Major Linke (*to the Prisoner*): Tell the Warden your full name.

Prisoner: Phillip Clark Morris.

Major Linke: You were convicted of being an accessory to fraud, right?

Prisoner: Well, yes. But like I said there's been a big misunderstanding.

Major Linke: You're damn right there has been. Whose accessory were you?

Prisoner: You mean who committed the fraud?

Major Linke: Yes.

Prisoner: Because I knew nothing about it...

Major Linke (*pressing*): Whose accessory were you convicted of being?

Prisoner: The first I heard about it was when he called me on his cell and said we had to pack up our stuff in a hurry and get out of the state...

Warden: Who called you and said that?

Prisoner: Why, Steven Russell, of course.

Warden (*incredulously*): Steven Russell?

Prisoner: Yes. (*Correcting himself*) I mean... yes, sir?

Warden (*pointing at him*): You're his boyfriend? You're that Phillip Morris?

Prisoner: Well, I was at the time, but that's not how things stand right now.

Warden (*loudly to Major Linke*): What in fuck's name is he doing here?

Major Linke: Sir, he's one of the 60 transferees that arrived here from Estelle. He's on the list. I mean I know he's not meant to be here, but he is meant to be here.

Warden: Of course, he's not meant to be here! What does that say at the very bottom of his file?

Major Linke: I know, sir, it's just…

Warden: What does it say?

Major Linke (*reading*): By order of TDCJ the offender is to be confined in a separate facility from Steven J. Russell, prisoner number 760259.

Warden: Do you know how I know what it says?

Major Linke: Because you issued the order?

Warden: And because I can fucking read!

Major Linke: Yes, sir.

Warden: So who is it around here that can't read and let this prisoner into my prison?

Major Linke: Sir, Estelle Unit should never have sent him over.

Prisoner: Can I go now, please?

Warden (*shouting at Phillip*): Stay exactly where you are. You don't move again until I say you can, do you hear me?

Prisoner: Yes, sir. It's just that...

Warden (*to Phillip*): Did I say you could talk?

Prisoner: No, sir. It's just I ...

Warden: Sit there and shut the fuck up. (*To Major Linke*) Yes, Estelle made an error, but how did we not spot this?

Major Linke: I guess because we didn't get the manifest until the transports arrived with the prisoners today. By then it was too late.

Warden: No. Not too late. Now is too late! Too late is assigning the known accomplice of a serial escapist held in administrative segregation to be the clerk to the Major in charge of administrative segregation! That's too fucking late! How did he get inside the perimeter?

Prisoner (*raising his hand*): May I please use the toilet?

Warden (*to Phillip*): No. You can't!

Prisoner (*to Lt. Herrera*): Um. It's kind of urgent.

Warden: I don't care if you piss yourself here in my office! You're not leaving my sight! (*To Major Linke*) Major, I want every person in and out of this prison checked against the list of individuals who are *persona non grata* at this facility, is that clear?

Major: Yes, sir. I'll draw up the list as soon as the meeting is over.

Warden (*pointing to Phillip*): Top of that list is Phillip fucking Morris.

Prisoner (*to Lt. Herrera*): I don't think I can hold it in much longer!

Warden: Listen to me, Morris. You are to be on the next transport out of here, do you hear me? You will be here for no longer than is absolutely necessary and if you're not on a transport by tomorrow morning then Major Linke here will be driving you back to Estelle himself, is that clear?

Prisoner (*crossing his legs, whining and nodding*): Uh huh.

Warden: If you value your life, and unless you particularly like pain, you will go absolutely nowhere near 12 building and you will make no attempt to contact Steven Russell while you are here. Is that absolutely, transparently, crystal clear?

Prisoner (*in a very high pitched voice*): Yes.

Warden (*to Lt. Herrera*): Lieutenant, take him to the nearest bathroom. Do not uncuff him and do not let him out of your sight.

Lt. Herrera: You want me to watch him pee?

Warden: I don't care if you have to hold his dick for him, you will not let him out of your sight!

Lt. Herrera (*to the prisoner*): Come here. (*Pointing out the door*) This way.

The Prisoner and Lt. Herrera leave the warden's office. As soon as the door closes behind them the Warden turns to Major Linke.

Warden (*pointing to Steven Russell's cell*): He had something to do with this! I know he did.

Major Linke: Russell?

Warden: Of course, Russell! Isn't it obvious? The man falsified his own medical records. You're telling me he can't pull off a stunt like this? Of course he can, he's done stuff like this dozens of times.

Major Linke: Sir, we've been watching him like a hawk.

Warden: I'm not saying I know how he did this, but I know he did.

The son-of-a-bitch.

Major Linke: Well, whatever he was planning, we've prevented it from happening.

Warden: Through luck! (*He reconsiders the situation*) Although, of course, Russell doesn't need to know that. Go and check on Morris and make sure he's not sucking off Lt. Herrera. I need to figure out how Russell did this.

Major Linke: Yes, sir.

The Major leaves Warden Alvarado's office. The Warden looks at the paperwork in front of him.

Warden: How in God's name did you do this, Russell?

Blackout in Warden Alvarado's Office.

The lights come on in Steven's cell. Steven is sitting on his bunk in front of his new typewriter. The Narrator is dictating to him.

Narrator: "Dear State Representative Terri Hodge,

I'm writing to you from 12 building at the Texas Department of Criminal Justice's Gabriel Unit.

My name is Steven Russell and I am currently serving a long sentence for a combination of insurance fraud... and escaping prison four times. I am not resident in your district, but I know you are a woman of integrity, which is why I am writing to ask for your help."

"In view of my past transgressions..."

Steven: Nice. Good word usage.

Narrator: Thanks. "In view of my past transgressions, Warden Alvarado, who now runs Gabriel Unit, has, understandably, introduced a number of additional security measures to keep me behind bars."

"I am writing to you with regard to one, and only one, of the measures he has implemented, which I believe contravenes state health and safety regulations and the rules laid down for public buildings by federal fire officials."

"Recently, Warden Alvarado placed a padlock on the outside of the sliding door to my cell. The key to the padlock is held in the guard's picket at the front of my building and must be signed for by any member of prison staff who needs it. This is a frequent occurrence because, although I am not allowed outside of the building in which I'm housed, I am allowed out of my cell on a more-than-daily basis to shower, recreate, receive visitors, meet with my attorney and members of the media."

"All other cells on my pod are opened electronically by a guard from the picket at the end of my row. Before the guard can remotely open my cell door, however, the padlock must first be unlocked and removed."

"My point is this. In the event of an emergency, be it a fire or flood, every other prisoner in my building will have their cell door opened remotely and automatically, allowing them to flee and muster within the secure grounds of the prison. All except for me."

"In order for me to be saved alongside the convicted killers I am surrounded by, a guard or fireman would have to brave the flames or water, obtain the key to my cell's padlock, fight his or her way to my cell, unlock the padlock, return back to the picket to open my cell, then potentially return to my cell a second time. Put simply, a rescuer would have to put their own life at risk to save mine."

"I have already filed a grievance, a complaint in everyday language, with the authorities here at Gabriel Unit asking that the padlock be removed. My grievance was denied and when I appealed the decision, my appeal was also denied."

"I would be grateful if you would take up my case with whomsoever you see fit, inside or outside of TDCJ, and thank you in advance for your assistance in this matter."

Steven: Wait a second... "TDCJ"... (*He continues typing*)... "in this matter". OK.

Narrator: And then:

"For your information I am forwarding copies of this letter to *The Houston Journal*, Warden Alvarado and the Livingston County Fire Department. Yours sincerely, Steven Russell."

Steven (*finishing typing*): Not bad. Even if I do say so myself.

Narrator: That should do the trick. I wish we could see the Warden's face when he reads his copy.

The lights in the cell start flicking on and off.

Steven (*looking up at the flashing ceiling light*): You might very well get that wish.

Narrator: I wonder what this is about?

Steven (*he turns his attention to the cell door*): I'm sure we're about to find out.

The noise of a padlock being unlocked can be heard.

Major Linke (*from outside*): OK. Roll 24!

Lt. Herrera (*repeating in the distance*): Rolling 24.

The door to Steven's cell opens and in steps Warden Alvarado.

Steven (*sounding pleasantly surprised*): Warden, we were just talking about you.

Warden: We, Russell? You and whom? (*Laughing*) Your boyfriend?

Steven: It doesn't matter. To what do I owe this pleasure? Would you like a drink? An Apple Martini perhaps?

Warden (*not moving*): You're slick Russell, I'll give you that...

Steven: Slick is my middle name. Only with a silent 'J' at the front.

Warden (*continuing*): ... but this time it didn't work.

Steven: It didn't?

Warden: Your little bum-buddy arrived here this morning.

Steven: Phillip? What a nice surprise. Will you be arranging a conjugal visit for the two of us?

Warden (*firmly*): He won't be staying.

Steven: Well that's a shame. The three of us could have sat in a circle and sung campfire songs.

Warden (*putting both his hands in his pockets*): I know how you did it, Russell. And it didn't work.

Steven: It sounds like it came awfully close to working though. Who knows, maybe it'll work next time?

Warden: There isn't going to be a next time. I guess you didn't believe me when I said you'd never see Phillip Morris again, but it wasn't a threat, Russell. It was the truth.

Steven: Well, I tell you what, why don't we just agree to disagree on that one.

Warden: I'm smarter than you are, Russell.

Steven: Of course you are. You're the smartest man I know. You know everything. Especially everything about me. I'm surprised you even waste your time talking to me. Isn't there some grandmaster chess tournament you should be taking part in? Or a MENSA meeting perhaps?

Warden (*leaving*): Always a pleasure, Russell. You'll have to excuse me, but I have tickets for a movie this evening. (*He turns back to face Steven*) You remember what movies are, don't you?

The Warden goes to leave.

Steven: I bet it's an arthouse movie, Warden. Am I right?

Narrator (*to Steven*): Give him the letter.

Steven: Oh, I almost forgot, I have something here for you.

Warden: Do you now?

The Warden stops, turns and takes the letter from Steven.

Steven: If you take it with you now, you'll save one of your trained monkeys having to bring it to you.

Warden: You can send as many letters as you like, Russell. It's not going to make one bit of difference. Animals like you need to be caged.

Steven: Well, I hope for your sake that Representative Hodge agrees with you, but I have a sneaking feeling she won't.

Warden (*heading out the cell*): Roll 24.

Lt. Herrera (*echoing from off-stage*): Rolling 24.

Steven's cell door closes.

Steven: What the fuck was all that about?

Narrator: The Estelle Unit had Phillip transferred here this morning?

Steven: That's what he said, but I thought someone decreed we were never to be housed in the same prison?

Narrator: Someone fucked up. Big time.

Steven (*getting excited*): Oh, my god, Phillip's here in Gabriel, right now!

Narrator: You're missing the point.

Steven: Which is?

Narrator: They think you had something to do with his coming here.

Steven: But this is the first I've heard of it.

Narrator: I know that. But they don't. And Alvarado just came here personally to tell you he'd foiled your plan to reunite with Phillip. A plan that never existed. You know what this means, right?

Steven: That I get to see Phillip?

Narrator (*angrily*): No! Quit thinking with your dick and use your brain. Phillip is currently being subjected to the same kind of security you are. Worse, probably. You can't get anywhere near him.

Steven: But he's so close. I wonder if I can see him?

Steven jumps up on the bed and looks out into the prison grounds, through the slit window above his bed.

Narrator: You're still missing the point.

Steven: What point?

Narrator: Oh, will you sit down? You can't see shit out of the window. The point is they think you had something to do with him coming here, but you didn't.

Steven (*getting down off of the bed*): Right?

Narrator: Which means it's working. We're getting inside Alvarado's head. He's accusing you of stuff you haven't done!

Steven: Wow. You're right.

Narrator: Yes.

Steven: But what about Phillip?

Narrator: Forget about Phillip. He might as well be a thousand miles away. That's the point of administrative segregation. We're segregated.

Steven (*sulking*): This sucks.

Narrator: No. This is awesome! Our plan is working. We just need to keep it up.

Steven: Well, what's next then?

Narrator: Steven, my good fellow. I think it's time we got some exercise.

ACT ONE

SCENE SEVEN

The lights come on to reveal three large recreation cages standing center-stage. Steven stands in the middle cage, looking lifeless and bored. The Narrator roams freely about the stage.

Narrator: It's glamorous, isn't it? Like being at the zoo. For inmates who are confined to exercising within their building, this is what recreation outside of your cell looks like. Usually, we wouldn't even bother. It's not compulsory and Major Young would much rather you give up your recreation rights in return for an extra food tray or an additional bar of soap. It's a hassle for them to have to cuff you, escort you to the cage, take the cuffs off, watch you do nothing, cuff you again and then take you back to your cell.

Everyone in here is entitled to recreation, which makes for a very dull working day. The more people that decline, the quicker they can get back to watching TV and eating donuts. It also reduces the chance they'll have shit thrown at them or get stabbed. Those are occupational hazards when you work with men who have nothing left to live for.

(To Steven) How are you doing in there, champ?

Steven: I'm slowly losing the will to live. We've been doing this now for two weeks with nothing to show for it.

Narrator: Patience, my dear fellow. Everything comes to he who waits.

Steven: Well, 'he who waits' is bored shitless.

Narrator: Do some exercise then.

Steven (*lifelessly*): Go fuck yourself.

Narrator: Slim pickings again?

Steven: The last one was mute and the other might as well have been. He could barely speak a word of English. It's like speed-dating in a straight bar.

Narrator (*to the audience*): Would you date a guy on death row? Believe it or not, a lot of women would and do. Many form long-distance relationships with inmates through letter-writing, which sometimes then leads to visits and occasionally even marriage. I don't know whether these women are looking for excitement, whether they think they can reform a bad boy or whether they just have a fetish for killers, but let me tell you a bit about some of the guys locked up here.

Over there (*he points to the left side of the audience*) in cell 20 is Bobby Fender, an ex-cop from a suburb of Houston. He is one sexy guy. Confident and with a cockiness that borders on arrogance. He denies any involvement in the murder of his wife, Francis Fender, yet was convicted of contracting her murder to two other men, also now on death row. Under Texas' Law of Parties, all three of them were found guilty of her murder and sentenced to death. Fender may not have pulled the trigger, but in the eyes of the law he is as responsible for his wife's death as the man or men that did.

Does he sound like a good catch? If he does, he has some special requirements that you should know about. You see, Bobby likes his women to defecate on him. He loves that shit! He also has a thing for chicks with dicks. Before getting locked up, Bobby would trawl through Houston's gay bars looking for transgender women who had both a vagina and a penis. I don't know if that's even possible. He told me that if I ever received a letter from someone fitting that description, I should pass it on to him. Needless to say, it's not something I've ever felt inclined to do.

Three doors down from Bobby, (*he points to the middle of the audience*) in cell 23, is Russell Lawrence Brewer. Now, if I ever make a list of my favorite inmates here, Lawrence Brewer would be at the very bottom of that list. He's what's known as a white supremacist and he, and two other members of the Aryan Brotherhood of Texas, were responsible for the murder of African-American James Byrd.

One day, Byrd accepted a ride from Brewer and his two pals who were out driving in their pick-up truck. Instead of driving him home however, they drove to a remote county road where Byrd was severely beaten and then urinated on. Brewer then decided it would be fun to chain Byrd by his ankles to the back of his pick-up truck, drive off, and drag him along for three miles. Forensic evidence suggests that Byrd was conscious for much of the ride, only dying when the truck finally hit a culvert, which decapitated him. His three killers then dumped Byrd's remains in front of an African-American church before driving off and attending a family barbecue.

Does he sound like good husband material?

The Narrator points to the right of the audience.

Across the hall from him, in cell 15, is George Rivas. George was serving seventeen life terms at Texas' Connelly Unit when he escaped with six other guys who worked in the prison's maintenance department. While on the run, Rivas conducted an armed robbery of a sporting goods store in Irving. A local police officer by the name of Aubrey Hawkins was the first respondent to the scene, reacting to a silent alarm that had been activated inside the store. Rivas shot him dead. When he was finally captured they sentenced him to death, rather than give him an eighteenth life term.

So, what's it to be, ladies? The alcoholic, redneck, white supremacist?

The dissatisfied husband with a fetish for hermaphroditic genitalia and scat? Or the cop-killing leader of the Texas Seven?

Then there's little ol' me, Steven Russell. A man who, despite the firearms and hand-to-hand combat training given to me and every other Texas law-enforcement officer, has never laid a finger on another human being.

And do you want to know what's really funny? The security arrangements for me are more rigorous than they are for any of those other guys! Somehow, I'm more of a threat to society? Please.

Major Linke brings in an inmate, Barney, and places him in the cage on the left-hand side of the stage. Like the other prisoners, Barney is dressed in prison-issued orange clothes. Barney turns his back to Major Linke, who removes his handcuffs.

Steven: Hey Barney.

Barney (*in a Filipino accent*): Hi Steven, how's it going? I read the piece about you in *The Prison Times*. You sure made fools of these clowns.

Steven: I aim to please, Barney. It's the least I can do for my adoring public.

Barney (*dumbly*): How come you got caught?

Steven: Well, what I didn't know was that the F.B.I. had placed a bug on me. They must have injected it into my neck here while I was sleeping.

Barney (*believing him*): Are you serious?

Lt. Herrera brings in another prisoner, Kelly, filling the cage to the right of the stage. Kelly is dressed in the same manner as Barney and Steven.

Steven (*still lying*): Yeah, it's some kind of experimental technology that NASA has developed. So when it came down to it, all they had to do was activate the satellite and hone in on me.

Barney: Wow.

Steven: I'm telling you Barney, it's the end of crime as we know it.

Barney: That's gonna suck! (*Pause*) The story didn't mention anything about a tracking device.

Steven: Because it's top secret, Barney! They hushed it up. They don't want the Russians getting their hands on that kind of technology.

Barney (*addressing the other prisoner*): Hi Kelly.

Kelly: Barney. Steven.

Barney: I heard you got gassed the other day.

Steven: Where did you learn to interact with people, Barney? The morgue?

Kelly (*a little hostile*): So, what if I did? What's it to you?

Barney: What happened, man? That stuff fucks with your eyes.

Kelly: They told me to come to the door. Wanted to move me to another cell, didn't they? Well, I refused.

Steven: That'll do it.

Barney: Why'd you do that, man? You know they're gonna use that shit on you.

Kelly: Because I'm fed up of this place, that's why! I hate it here. I'd rather be anywhere than here.

Steven: Right? It looks nothing like the brochure.

Barney: I know what you mean, man. I'd give anything to be back in general population. I hate this ad seg shit.

Steven: Barney, what did you do to get moved in here? Right now I'm finding it hard to imagine you doing anything, to be perfectly honest.

Barney: It was a set-up, man. They found an ounce of hash in my cell.

Steven: They put you in here for an ounce?

Barney: That and the other three ounces I sold to guys on my row.

Steven: So you had four ounces, then?

Barney: They only put me in here because I was undercutting the guard who usually supplies my row. He was angry when he found out what I was doing.

Steven: Why would you undercut him?

Barney: Because I just found it. Turns out it was actually his stock. He must have left it in my cell accidentally.

Steven: You sold a guard's drugs and undercut him in the process? You're braver than I thought.

Barney: It seemed like a good idea at the time. But since they put me in here I'm not so sure it was a smart move.

Kelly: Quit complaining, you'll be back in general population in a week or two.

Barney: I don't think I can wait that long. I hate it here. I don't like being on my own. Steven, you're really smart, can't you think of a way to get me back to general population? I'm losing my mind in here.

Steven: And you really don't have any extra to spare, do you?

Narrator: I smell an opportunity.

Steven (*to the Narrator*): No, I think it's just Barney.

Kelly: If you're so smart, Steven, think of a way to get me transferred to another prison while you're at it.

Narrator: Bingo!

Steven (*intrigued*): Let me get this straight. Barney, you want to get transferred back to general population?

Barney: More than anything in the world.

Steven: And Kelly, you just want out of here and you don't care where you get sent, so long as it's not Gabriel Unit.

Kelly: It could be the Moon for all I care.

Steven: Although somewhere with oxygen would be preferable, right?

Narrator (*excitedly*): And we want to edge our way just that little bit further into Alvarado's increasingly warped mind.

Barney: So, Steven, have you got any ideas?

Steven (*he puts his hand to his head*): Give me a minute, I'm thinking.

Narrator (*laughing*): No you're not! You already know what to do. You're just delaying for dramatic effect!

Steven claps his hands.

Steven: I've got it!

Kelly: Well, what is it?

Barney: Tell us, Steven. What's your plan?

Steven: I have a plan, but there are consequences for both of you.

Kelly: What kind of consequences?

Steven (*turning to Kelly*): Kelly, you are going to have to take a disciplinary in order for this scheme to work.

Kelly (*standing more upright*): Is that it? That don't bother me. I'm never getting out anyway. What's the worst they can do to me?

Steven: And Barney, you have to be prepared to do some snitching.

Barney: What? I don't know, Steven. I'm no snitch.

Steven: Well, the good news is you only have to snitch on us. And we don't mind. Plus neither one of us is going to tell anyone that you snitched on us.

Barney: Oh. I could do that.

Kelly: What's the idea, Steven?

Steven: It's simple. Barney, you are going to snitch on Kelly and me to Warden Alvarado. Tell him that you overheard us today, planning to escape together. But tell him you'll only share the details if he promises to transfer you back to general population.

Barney: You two are planning to escape?

Steven: As far as you're concerned, Barney, yes we are. (*He turns to Kelly*) Kelly, you are going to have to buy some hacksaw blades from someone in maintenance.

He turns back to Barney.

This is how it will go down: Alvarado will readily agree to move you back to general population because he is shit-scared about his reputation. By mentioning me you can be certain he'll take the threat of escape seriously, which is why he'll agree to your terms. I reckon you'll be back in general population before sunset tomorrow.

He turns back to Kelly.

Kelly, things will be a bit slower for you, but you'll still make it out of here. Once Barney's told Alvarado about our plans, they're certain to search both of our cells. Although they'll find nothing in mine, in yours they'll find the hacksaw blades. When they question you, deny everything. You and I never had a plan to escape and you don't know how the blades came to be in your cell. They won't believe you, but coupled with me denying any involvement in an escape plan, they'll only be able to get you for possession of contraband. That's the disciplinary you'll face. And after your disciplinary they'll transfer you to another prison because Alvarado won't want you in the same jail as me.

What do you think? Are you guys in?

Narrator: It's foolproof. (*He points at Barney*) It may even be Barney-proof!

Kelly: It sounds good to me. I'm in.

Barney: Yeah, count me in too.

Steven: Then it's on.

The recreation cages are thrown into half-light. Steven is let out of his cage and taken back to his cell. The other inmates are taken offstage along with all three cages. A spotlight falls on the Narrator.

Narrator (*to the audience*): And just as we predicted, Alvarado moved Barney back to general population and in return Barney told the warden about Kelly's and my plan for a 'great escape'.

Both of our cells were duly searched and while the prison guards found nothing in ours, they found three hacksaw blades in Kelly's.

Kelly was transferred to a prison in Northern Texas shortly after finishing his disciplinary here at Gabriel and everyone got what they wanted.

Of course, Warden Alvarado thought he had foiled another of Steven Russell's great escape plans, but since there was nothing they could specifically pin on us, we were sitting pretty, having just thrown a little bit more sand in the machine.

The lights go on in Steven's cell, revealing Steven on his bed and Warden Alvarado at his door. Steven is doing the New York Times crossword.

Warden: We moved your friend Kelly to another unit today, Russell.

Steven: Thanks, Warden. I'm sure he'll be much happier there.

Warden: So, I'm afraid he's not going to be of much use to you.

Steven: That's a pity. Out of interest, Warden, on a scale of 1 to 10, how clever do you think you are for foiling yet another of my Machiavellian schemes?

Warden: Clever enough to outsmart you. That's all I need to be.

Steven: You're too modest. You're so impressive I bet you go home each night and touch yourself in front of a mirror.

Warden: Save your small talk for your visitor, Russell.

The Narrator walks up to Steven's cell.

Narrator: We have a visitor?

Steven (*to the Warden*): And you came here to tell me in person? Is it Harry Houdini? He's been writing to me for ages asking for some tips.

Warden: Actually, Russell, somewhat improbably it's your daughter.

ACT ONE

SCENE EIGHT

The spotlight falls, center stage, on the Narrator.

Narrator (*to the audience*): Long before gay men and women were finally allowed to adopt, a good deal of us gay folk fathered children the old-fashioned way. Which is to say that society pressured us into marriage and thereafter into the baby game. I wasn't immune to that pressure. I wanted to be a family man like the guys at my church, my colleagues in law enforcement, and my neighbors.

But, after a few years of sucking dick on the side, it became clear to me that the whole pretending-to-be-heterosexual thing wasn't really going to work out. It wasn't fair to my wife, who deserved someone that loved her totally. It wasn't fair to me. And it wasn't fair to our beautiful daughter, Sally.

The lights come on in the visitors' area. The Narrator is absent for his daughter's visit, instead sitting in Steven's cell. Major Linke sits Steven down in a chair on one side of the Plexiglas and removes his handcuffs. Sally is waiting for him, sitting on the chair on the other side. She is wearing blue jeans and a yellow top. Each of them picks up a telephone receiver to converse.

Steven: Well, this is a lovely surprise.

Sally: Hi, Dad. How are you? I've missed you.

Steven: I'm good. I've missed you too, sweetheart. I had no idea you were coming. You should have written and told me. I could have baked a cake or something.

Sally: It was kind of a last-minute thing. A girl I know at the airline asked if I could cover a shift for her. She currently has water pouring through the ceiling of her condo. She needed a plumber and to get that whole mess sorted so, unexpectedly, I found myself in Houston with nothing to do. I fly back east tomorrow.

Steven: Did you rent a car?

Sally: No, I walked here from Houston. Of course, I hired a car.

Steven: Well, it's great to see you.

Sally: How was Florida?

Steven: Oh. How did you hear about that?

Sally: Mom told me.

Steven: And how is your mother?

Sally: As perplexed as I am that, although you seem capable of escaping prison, not that I'm condoning it in any way, you don't seem to be able to prevent yourself from getting put back in here.

Steven: It's a long story. Escaping sure made a lot of sense at the time.

Sally: Don't get me wrong. It's a great conversation starter when I meet new crewmembers. "Hi, my name's Jessica." "Hi, I'm Sally." "I haven't seen you before, how long have you been with the airline?" "Four years." "Oh you're a newbie." "Yes, what's that you're reading?" "Oh, it's an article on my father who's just escaped from prison."

It gives me kudos, you know? Although I saw a few first-class passengers clutch their wallets tighter when they overheard. I'm sure most people realize criminality isn't hereditary, but for some reason telling them your father's in a maximum-security prison doesn't engender trust in people. Not in the Bible Belt. It's a bit like the gay-dad thing. It works better on the coasts.

Steven: How is the gay-dad thing for you these days?

Sally: For me? You know Mom and I are cool with it. She was cooler with it after the divorce, of course. And after she met Frank. I have more of a problem with the prison-dad thing. (*She pauses*) Because it means you won't be able to come to my wedding...

Steven: You're getting married??

Sally: Yeah, you might know the guy actually. He did five years in one of the units you were in.

Steven (*standing*): He did what?!!

Sally (*laughing*): No, I'm not getting married! (*Steven sits down again*) Well, I mean, hopefully one day, yes, but not anytime soon. But even if that day comes you won't be able to come, will you? Who's going to give me away?

Steven: Your mother? The groom's father?

Sally: Aren't you going to miss all that? Because I will.

Steven: Of course, I am, but... What's brought all this on?

Sally: Oh, nothing. I was leafing through some magazines and journals in a terminal the other day and I came across this story about a guy called Nick Leeson. He was the trader who brought down Barings, the British bank. He lost $1.4bn of their money and ended up in a prison in Singapore. Anyway, it wasn't so much Nick Leeson I was interested in, but his wife, Lisa. She ended up getting a job with Virgin Atlantic Airways so she could visit him often. And more cheaply, I suppose. Her story sounded a bit like mine.

Steven: You didn't get a job with Delta just so you could visit me.

Sally: No, but it makes it easier. Anyway, there's more. After coming across the Nick Leeson article, I remembered the last time I came to see you. I stopped for gas about five miles from here, on the way back to the airport. Well, you know how the visitors' area vending machines only accept one-dollar coins? And how the front gate will only let you bring in twenty bucks' worth?

Steven: Only too well.

Sally: Have you any idea how difficult it is to get dollar coins? I had to go to three banks before I found one that would sell me a twenty-dollar roll.

Steven: How much did it cost?

Sally: Twenty bucks, smartass! Don't try and make me laugh, I'm being serious. Anyway, after filling up, when I went inside to get a soda, the cashier noticed I had a lot of dollar coins left over from visiting you and asked if she could buy them from me.

Steven: And you put two and two together and assumed that she's either married to or dating someone in here?

Sally: Why else would she need the coins?

Steven: There could be any number of reasons? The mints put presidents' heads on them because people collect them.

Sally: She was in her early twenties. She wasn't a ... (*she searches for the right word*) ...numismatist.

Steven (*smiling*): Oh, you know you make Daddy proud when you use long words.

Sally: Whatever. Yes, she could have wanted them for any number of reasons, but one of those reasons might be because her husband or boyfriend is locked up in here and she moved here to be with him and took a job at that gas station.

Steven: How much did you charge her?

Sally: For the dollar coins? Well, you know I knew she needed them so, like, a buck twenty each.

They laugh.

Steven: Are you trying to make me feel guilty, because the guilt thing gets old after a while?

Sally: I'm just shooting the breeze with you. I'm not trying to make you feel guilty. (*She pauses*) Do you feel guilty?

Steven: I don't have time for guilt. I know that sounds harsh, but I really don't. I could sit in my cell at night and think about all your birthdays that I've missed. All the Christmases and Halloweens... all that stuff. And you're right, one day you're going to meet a terrific guy and I'm going to miss what should be the happiest day of your life. But there's nothing I can do about that. So, what's the point feeling guilty? It serves no purpose. Guilt is like a flashing red light that's meant to make sure you do the right thing next time. There isn't going to be a next time for me. So what's the point?

Sally: Is that why you escaped? To give yourself a 'next time'?

Steven: I did it because I could. And because I wanted to see Phillip.

Sally: He must be pretty special.

Steven: It takes someone pretty special to love a man like me.

Sally: Oh, I know.

Steven: I don't know when I'll see him again. They'll let him out eventually, but I don't know when that will be.

Sally: Hello? You don't know when you'll see me again.

Steven: It better be damned soon or the next time I get out of here I'm gonna kick your ass.

They laugh.

Sally: And then you'd be back in here with an assault conviction.

Steven: Wouldn't it be crazy if I just showed up on one of your flights one day?

Sally: 'Crazy' would be one word to describe it. 'Illegal' would be another. I'm not sure how the authorities would feel about me harboring a known fugitive. Even in economy.

Steven: Sweetheart, I'd be up front in first class.

Sally: I've never asked you this before, because I didn't want to upset either one of us, but are they ever going to let you out? I mean, legitimately?

Steven (*sighing*): I don't know.

Sally: I guess if you thought they would, you wouldn't have escaped again, right?

Steven: They might. Eventually.

Sally: I know these conversations are recorded, but are you planning on escaping again?

Steven: I want you to look at me very carefully, OK?

Sally: OK.

Steven: Now, ask me again.

Sally: Dad, are you planning on escaping again?

Steven (*shaking his head*): Yes.

Sally: Well, that'll be something to look forward to, I suppose. Oh, that reminds me, I have something for you.

Steven: You do?

Sally: Well, I do and I don't. I have a book for you to read. I knew they wouldn't let me bring it in, but for some reason I still brought it with me. It's in the rental, in the parking lot. I'll put it in the post as soon as I get home. It's called *Catch Me If You Can*. It's about a man called Frank Abagnale. He started off life as a forger and later passed himself off as an airline pilot, a doctor and then a lawyer. He sounds just as crazy as you. Another crewmember was reading it and when I told them all about you they said I should read it and then pass it on.

Steven: He passed himself off as a pilot? Could he actually fly?

Sally: He couldn't fly, he had no medical training and no law degree. Yet each time he fooled everyone around him into believing he was the real deal. He did more than 250 flights for Pan Am before they realized what he was doing.

Steven: He must have balls as big as mine.

Sally: Dad! Gross.

Steven: Oh, sorry.

Sally: That's a mental image I could do without. Anyway, when he was eventually caught, in France in 1969, twelve countries sought his extradition for bank fraud and forgery. Only, like you, he wasn't too keen on serving time in prison.

Steven: He escaped?

Sally: Twice! When the French deported him back to America he escaped the VC-10 he was flown in on while it was taxiing to a stand at JFK. Years later, when he was in prison in Virginia, he escaped by impersonating an undercover prison inspector.

Steven: You mean he pulled that one before I did?

Sally: The lady that gave me the book has a cousin who works for a literary agent, or something. She said Stephen Spielberg's bought the movie rights and it's going to be a film.

Steven (*intrigued*): Really?

Sally: So, maybe that's something you should think about.

Steven: I think you might be on to something.

Sally: There's also a small part of me that thinks that trying to write a book might keep you out of trouble for a while.

Steven: Stranger things have happened.

Sally: You will stay out of trouble, won't you Dad? For me?

Steven (*nodding his head*): Of course I won't, baby.

ACT ONE

SCENE NINE

The lights go on in Steven's cell. The Narrator is lying on Steven's bed with his legs crossed and his hands behind his head. Steven returns excitedly to his cell. His cuffs are removed as he re-enters.

Narrator: How is our little buttercup?

Steven: She's pregnant.

Narrator: What?

Steven: Twins. Some Mexican guy's the father.

Narrator: No, she's not!

Steven: Of course she isn't, but I have exciting, exciting news!

Narrator: What is it? What did she say?

Steven: We're going to write a book!

Narrator: We are?

Steven: Oh come on, you already knew that! Or it might be a film. Or a book that gets made into a film.

Narrator: And why would we want to do that?

Steven: Because nothing would piss off Warden Alvarado more than having our story out there. In hardback. In paperback! On bookshelves, in libraries, in movie theaters, on TV screens! Think of what that would do to him! It would drive him over the edge!

Narrator: And it would make us famous!

Steven: We wouldn't be in it for the fame.

Narrator: Wouldn't we?

Steven: No, we'd be in it for the money.

Narrator: Both would go a long way here. A little bit of star treatment certainly wouldn't go amiss.

Steven: And it would drive Alvarado mad! He didn't even want us to be interviewed by *The Houston Journal*. Imagine how he'd feel if our life story was showing at the local multiplex. Or if there was a billboard advertising a film about us on his journey home. A film about how we made fools out of the Texas Department of Criminal Justice!

Narrator: OK. I'm sold. But tell me why anyone would be interested in spending a Friday or Saturday night watching one hundred and one minutes about us?

Steven: Because they've already published Frank Abagnale's story and they're making it into a film!

Narrator: Who?

Steven: Some conman who only escaped custody twice.

Narrator: Twice? (*Dismissively*) Is he blind or something? He sounds like an amateur.

Steven: He's a charlatan. A freshman at the school of prison escapes. We're twice the man he is.

Narrator: There's only one small problem with your plan…

Steven: What's that?

Narrator: We can't write for shit!

Steven: We won't need to.

Narrator: So, how's your brilliant plan going to work then?

Steven: We'll get someone to write it for us!

Narrator: Who?

Steven: A writer.

Narrator: No shit.

Steven: Well, a journalist then. I don't know. Maybe one that's already written about us.

Narrator: Like that guy from *The Houston Journal?* McVicker? That was his name, right?

Steven: Yes! Steve McVicker.

Narrator: Has he ever written a book before?

Steven: I don't know. But how difficult can it be? It's just words on a page. He's done that loads of times in newspapers. Books just have more pages. And he can write, can't he?

Narrator: Why would he do it?

Steven: Because he'll make money. Hello! People would buy the book. We're really interesting! The public love all that true crime stuff. They'll lap it up. And if they do, maybe someone will make it into a film. Someone like Steven Spielberg!

Narrator: Steven Spielberg is a lot like Steven Spielberg.

Steven: Yes, but there are other Hollywood directors as well.

Narrator: Would we get to fly in a wicker basket on the front of a bicycle?

Steven: Only if we break the habit of a lifetime and take lots of drugs.

Narrator: This Frank Abagnale character...

Steven: What about him?

Narrator: ... Was he gay or straight?

Steven: Who knows? Who cares? I mean, maybe Jack the Ripper was some misogynist, Victorian-era homosexual. Maybe that's why he killed all those hookers. Ours wouldn't be a book about sex, or about Phillip, it would be about a modern-day criminal genius!

Narrator: Sex sells, Steven. You know that. You bought those Calvin Klein jockey shorts solely because of the model on the packaging.

Steven: For the price I paid, I assumed he came free with them. Anyway, a director would skip over the gay stuff. Oh, my god! They'll probably get some really hot leading man to play me!

Narrator: Like Brad Pitt.

Steven: Mmm... Brad Pitt.

Narrator: Knowing our luck we'll probably end up with some fat ass like John Goodman or John Candy...

Steven: John Candy died four years ago.

Narrator: He did? Shit. That means we're stuck with Goodman.

Steven: It's a good idea though, right? I mean we can pull all kinds of stunts in this joint to wind up Alvarado, but this would take things to an entirely different level.

Narrator: Can you remember all the dates that stuff happened?

Steven (*proudly*): I have a photographic memory.

Narrator: That's what you tell people, but is it true?

Steven: It doesn't matter. McVicker, or whoever it is, will be able to look up all that shit. He'll have access to all the press clippings and databases. What do you say? Are we in?

The Narrator stands up.

Narrator: We're in!

Steven spits on his hand and offers it to the Narrator who does the same. They shake hands.

Narrator: Have you still got McVicker's address?

Steven: Right over here.

Narrator: Well then, let's write him a letter!

Steven and the Narrator sit down on his bed, Steven in front of his typewriter and the Narrator next to him. Steven starts typing while the Narrator reads the text in his head. As they do this a Beautiful Woman walks on from stage left. She is holding up a sign that reads '1998.' She walks to center stage, poses with the sign and smiles.

Steven: Who the fuck is that?

The Beautiful Woman walks to stand stage right.

Narrator: She's so everyone knows what year it is.

Steven: Is she in my mind too?

Narrator: She sure is. Do you know how long it's going to take to write a book in here? Even assuming McVicker says yes, we're going to have to get all that information out of your head, into his, and onto paper. That's going to take a while. If this were a film we'd cut to a montage right about now.

Steven: How long will it take?

Narrator (*nonchalantly*): At a wild guess, I'd say about four years, two months and twelve days.

Steven: Four years?

Narrator: Yeah. You got somewhere else you need to be?

Steven: I guess not. Will it be worth it?

Narrator: Oh, it'll be worth it! And don't worry there's lots we can do to fuck with Alvarado's head in the meantime. And there's another benefit to all of this as well. By the time we've finished, you'll be able to type with more than just two fingers. Finish that letter to McVicker and I'll be back in a bit.

The Narrator moves to the front, center stage, to address the audience. Steven types away in the background.

Narrator: By the end of 1998 our war with Warden Alvarado was progressing well. Steve McVicker agreed to write a book based on our prison exploits and, thanks to Representative Terri Hodge, the padlock on our cell door was removed.

Things with Phillip on the other hand, had soured. Towards the end of the year he wrote to us and blamed us for everything bad that had happened in his life. He reacted to the idea of our book with indifference, seeing as it wouldn't have any immediate effect on him.

The Beautiful Woman exits stage right with her sign.

Narrator: There was little that Steven could do for Phillip, given we were in separate prisons, miles apart, and especially given Phillip's attitude. Slowly, Steven felt less and less inclined to even try. Soon 1999 was upon us…

The Beautiful Woman re-emerges from stage left holding a new sign that reads '1999'.

Narrator: The New Year brought the news that Georgia Russell, the woman who adopted us and who was to all intents and purposes our mother, had died of a cardiac arrest. It would be nice to think that Warden Alvarado took no pleasure in relaying the news to us, but sadly that wasn't the case. He refused permission for us to leave Gabriel Unit to attend her funeral. All of which made us more determined to continue our work with McVicker.

Steven (*reading from a new letter he is typing to McVicker*): "The first thing you need to know is the timing of my escapes was always deliberate. Nothing I did was opportunistic. Everything was planned down to the last detail."

"My first escape took place on Friday 13, March 1992. The second on Friday 13, July 1996. The third occurred on Friday 13, December 1996 and my last, and I hope you're noticing a pattern here, happened as I was wheeled out of that hospice on Friday 13, March 1998."

"Why did I always escape on Friday the 13th? Do I believe that's a lucky day for me? Not at all. I subscribe to the school of thought that says the harder people work the luckier they seem to get. I study people. I studied the guards and applied logic to everything they did and worked out why they did things a certain way. That's how I escaped and how I was able to plan exactly when I escaped. When I walked out of that hospice last year and into the taxi that was meant to take me away for experimental AIDS treatment, I instead went to a local car lot where I'd arranged for a brand new Jeep Cherokee to be waiting for me. Planning is everything."

"So why Friday the 13th? I suppose it was fate. Even though I didn't know Phillip when I escaped prison the first time, March 13, the exact date of my first and last escapes, happens to be Phillip's birthday. That's how, when we met, I knew we were meant to be together. It was fate. Or at least that's what I thought at the time."

Steven folds the letter, puts it in an envelope and posts it through the letterbox of his cell.

Narrator (*to the audience*): To say that things with Phillip were complex at this point would be an understatement. When Phillip wrote to us it was rarely more than a diatribe of negativity and blame that was self-serving and self-absorbed.

On an almost daily basis, however, in letters to McVicker, we were reliving all the good times we'd shared with Phillip. Then, midway through 1999, something happened. Something almost imperceptible, but something profound.

You see, in administrative segregation inmates aren't just physically confined, they're subject to sensory confinement as well. When loved ones come and visit ad seg inmates don't get to kiss them or hold their hand. The best you can do is hold your hand up to the Plexiglas, wait for your significant other to do the same and imagine the two of you are touching.

We hadn't had physical contact with another human being since being assigned to administrative segregation. Until one day in 1999, when we were out exercising in those big old cages you saw earlier, and a new inmate, a Latino by the name of Tommy, was placed in the cage next to ours.

Tommy was a beautiful young man, a Mexican gang-member who'd been moved to our wing as a precautionary measure until he could be transferred to another prison. We made eye contact and I guess he either knew or worked out we were gay. Without saying a word we both reached out our hands from our respective cages.

Now, those cages are deliberately spaced far enough apart that it's impossible for inmates to touch or harm one another, but somehow, by standing on tiptoe and stretching as hard as we both could, our fingers managed to touch. It felt like electricity.

Although he was transferred out of Gabriel Unit a few months later, the memory of that contact stayed with us. And, as it lingered, our attachment to Phillip grew weaker.

He clears his throat.

McVicker visited us every Sunday morning that year, and after he'd gone Steven and I would come back to our cell and type out long answers to the questions he'd posed. Mailing these to him had its consequences, since all of our incoming and outgoing mail was heavily vetted, but there was no way around it. Writing the book meant inadvertently sharing a lot of information with Warden Alvarado and his goons. What was interesting to us, however, was just how little he knew about our previous exploits.

The Beautiful Woman exits stage right.

ACT ONE

SCENE TEN

The lights go on in Warden Alvarado's office. The Warden is sitting at his desk. There is a knock at the door and Major Linke enters the room.

Major Linke: Sir, I need to talk to you about Steven Russell.

Warden: What is it?

Major Linke: Three things, sir. The most immediate of which is that one of the periodic searches you ordered us to conduct on his cell turned up a bottle of green dye in his room.

Warden: Green dye? Like the one he used to make those doctor's scrubs back in '96?

Major Linke: Not exactly. He used pen ink that time. This was legitimate textile dye.

Warden: Well, how in God's name did that find its way into my unit? Did he get it from laundry?

Major Linke: I don't know, sir.

Warden: Do you trust your men, Major?

Major Linke: Most of them.

Warden: Because something like that can only get in here if one or more of your men was complicit in letting it enter.

Major Linke: It could have come from one of the inmate's visitors.

Warden: Are you suggesting the visitation area isn't secure, Major?

Major Linke: No, sir.

Warden: Then take my word for it. It came from one of your men. Draw me up a list of who might be responsible and I'll speak to them one by one.

Major Linke: Yes, sir.

Warden: What did Russell have to say when you found it?

Major Linke: He said he didn't like the décor in his cell.

Warden: He only knows how to lie, Major.

Major Linke: Yes, sir. Shall I start disciplinary proceedings?

Warden: And what would be the point of that?

Major Linke: It's clearly contraband.

Warden: He's not going anywhere. A disciplinary would just show up on his record and lead the press to ask more questions than they already do. What else was it?

Major Linke: He's requested that Phillip Morris be put on his visitation list.

Warden: Morris? On his visitation list?

Major Linke: Yes, sir.

Warden: The same Phillip Morris currently incarcerated in the queers' wing of Hughes Unit?

Major Linke: Yes, sir.

Warden: What the fuck is he playing at?

Major Linke: I don't know. It seems harmless, but I thought I'd clear it by…

Warden: What's harmless about it?

Major Linke: You won't allow it?

Warden: Of course, I won't allow it. Morris may not be able to visit him, but that is beside the point. That man is banned from this facility while Russell is here.

Major Linke: Sir, what reason will we give in denying the request?

Warden: Don't give a reason. What's he going to do? File another grievance? He's filed more than fifty in the past year. How many of them have been upheld, Major?

Major Linke: None, sir.

Warden: Exactly. Deny the request and when you're done with that get a message to Warden Straw at the Hughes Unit and tell him to keep a close eye on Morris. Something may be up.

Major Linke: Yes, sir.

Warden: What was the third thing, Major?

Major Linke: Friday the 13th, sir.

Warden: Unlucky for some. What about it?

Major Linke: All four of Russell's escapes have been on Friday the 13th.

Warden (*pausing*): What did you just say?

Major Linke: I don't know why we've never made the connection before, but in one of the letters he sent to that reporter, he spells it all out. I went through his record and the two escapes he was convicted of both happened on a Friday the 13th. I checked the arrest records for the two other escapes he committed and both of them happened on a Friday the 13th as well.

Warden: Why the hell have we never connected the dots before?

Major Linke: I think because he was only convicted of two...

Warden: It's a rhetorical question!

Major Linke: Yes, sir. But there's good news.

Warden: How can there be good news? He's made us look like chumps and he's going to tell the world about it in a fucking book.

Major Linke: I did some research, sir and although there is at least one Friday the 13th a year, and at most three, there's only one each in 1999 and 2000. And the one for 1999 has already passed.

Warden: Really?

Major Linke: Yes, sir. August 13.

Warden: When's the next one?

Major Linke: October 13, 2000.

Warden: You're sure there isn't one before then?

Major Linke: No, sir. I had Betsy in administration check every month between now and then. She has one of those day-to-a-page-diaries with that little chart right in the back that tells you what day of the week dates next year will be.

Warden: Betsy in administration? Betsy Murray?

Major Linke: Yes, sir.

Warden: A woman so longsighted she backed into the guards' picket in the employee parking lot.

Major Linke: That's the one.

Warden: Bring me a copy of the letter Russell sent to McVicker.

Major Linke: Right away, sir.

Warden: And a calendar.

Major Linke: Yes, sir.

Warden: And a loaded gun.

Major Linke: A gun, sir? Why would you need…

Warden: Because I can't believe we missed this, Major, and I want to shoot myself!

ACT ONE

SCENE ELEVEN

A spotlight shines on the Narrator, who is center stage again. The lights come on in Steven's cell. Steven is listening to the radio on his bed.

Narrator: When the alarm clock struck midnight on December 31, 1999, we welcomed the new millennium listening to *KUHF*, even though strictly speaking the new millennium wouldn't start until January 1, 2001. Residents of the houses situated on the banks of nearby Lake Houston let off fireworks, the echoes of which we could hear in our cell.

The Beautiful Woman enters from stage left carrying a card with the year '2000' written on it.

Narrator: Early in 2000, we finally gave in to our daughter and saw a psychiatrist who, to the surprise of no one, diagnosed us with obsessive-compulsive disorder.

We continued to meet and correspond with Steve McVicker and slowly but surely he mapped out a book proposal that could be sent to the publishing industry.

In August, I was finally charged with my December 1996 escape. It was case number 19,856-C, a crime they'd been happy to overlook when they thought I was dying.

I was given an unprecedented sentence of 99 years! 99 years for walking out the prison's front door in a pair of prison scrubs dyed green using Magic Markers! People serve less time for murder. It was beyond outrageous.

It meant that if I served all my sentences sequentially, I would not be released until July 12, in the year 2140, or just in time to celebrate my 183rd birthday.

But, rather than letting small details like that get me down, I sent a note to Warden Alvarado explaining how I looked forward to many more joy-filled years with him.

Then along came October...

Major Linke comes to the door of Steven Russell's cell.

Major Linke: Come to the door.

Steven: I have a name you know? It's Steven. (*He is duly handcuffed through the cell door's letterbox*) But if you're nice I'll let you call me Vanessa.

Major Linke: He's secured.

Steven (*turning and sniffing the air*): Is that you I can smell, Warden Alvarado?

The cell door slides open and the Warden walks in. Steven Russell sits down on his bunk and looks at the Warden who leans on the cell wall near the door.

Warden: Good evening, Steven. I hope I haven't disturbed your writing.

Steven: Not at all. Did you bring donuts and coffee?

Narrator (*to Steven*): From the look of him, I think he ate all the donuts already.

Warden: You must be wondering why I'm here.

Steven: I have a feeling you're going to tell me.

Warden: Do you know what day it is today?

Steven: It's a Saturday. I believe it is October 7 in the year of our Lord 2000.

Warden: Very good. And do you know what the coming Friday will be?

Steven: Independence Day?

Warden: No, Russell. It's going to be Friday the 13th.

Steven (*smiling*): Is it now?

Warden: So, just in case you were thinking of getting any, shall we say 'fresh air', we are going to do things a little differently over the next nine days.

Steven: Oh, you know me, warden, I love a challenge.

Warden: From now until the 15th your property is going to be removed from your cell and inventoried by the property officer every other day. It will only be returned to you the day after everything has been noted and logged.

You will be videoed during this time whenever you leave your cell, even if it's just to go to the shower.

Steven: Which fool is going to have to watch all that footage? Not you, I hope, Warden.

Warden: You are going to be rotated to a different cell every other day, and every time you leave and enter a cell a lieutenant and two other officers will accompany you.

Steven: One of whom will presumably be holding the video camera? Warden, which do you think is my best side? The left or the right?

Warden: On the 9th of any month containing a Friday the 13th you will be given a new mattress, new sheets, new blankets, a new pillow, a new pair of state shoes and boxers. Every item being replaced will be thoroughly checked for contraband.

From 6 p.m. on the 12th of the month, on the hour and every hour until the 16th, in addition to the 30-minute cell visuals you are currently subjected to, the duty captain will be required to visually confirm you are in your cell.

Steven: How will he be able to tell that I'm not a cyborg just pretending to be me?

Warden: Furthermore, twice on any Friday the 13th, the Major in charge of administrative segregation will be required to visit your cell to personally confirm you are still here.

Steven: Warden, I'm blushing.

Warden: Finally, on each Friday the 13th, you will be taken to the Assistant Warden and interviewed by him.

Steven: Will snacks be provided? I presume the idea there is that my 'accomplices' will think you've found out our plan and that I'm snitching on them, right? Do you think that would put them off? Will everything you've described be enough to keep me here?

Warden: I just want you to know that you are not going anywhere on my watch.

Steven: Did it ever occur to you that all the extra visits to my cell, all that extra attention, is just providing more opportunity for one of your guards to slip up or deliver something to me? Are you going to give them a loyalty bonus for every Friday the 13th that passes when I don't escape?

Warden: The extra attention is designed to make sure that you slip up, Russell. That you forget something. Because as smart as you think you are, you're human like the rest of us and you make mistakes too.

The Warden goes to leave.

Steven: Did you know, there were three Friday the 13ths in 1998, even though it wasn't a leap year? (*The Warden turns around*). The first occurred in February, when I was planning my fourth escape, the second occurred in March when I checked out of the hospice… and the third took place in November, by which time I was back here and you were Warden.

And yet you didn't have any of these precautions in place then, did you? They were also absent in August last year, which also had a Friday the 13th. Which leads me to believe you didn't even realize that every time I walked out of one of your prisons it was always on the same day. So, the only reason you know now is because I said as much in a letter to Steve McVicker.

Warden: Like I said, you're human and you make mistakes.

Steven: How stupid did you feel when you finally found out?

Warden: Try and escape, Russell. I dare you. McVicker's book will sell more copies if you're dead.

Steven: I think it's going to sell just enough copies as it is. The question is, does the story need one more escape? Something big to finish on?

Warden: How about we finish it with a bang?

Steven: How about I send you a postcard from Times Square?

Warden: No one is going to read your book, Russell. I'd be surprised if it even gets published.

Steven: Well, we'll have to agree to disagree on that one. See, there's a literary agent in New York who thinks it will sell just fine.

Warden: You're bluffing.

Steven: The agent's name is Peter Steinberg. Why don't you go look him up?

Warden: Enjoy your Friday the 13th, Russell.

Steven: You too, Warden.

Warden Alvarado walks out of Steven's cell. The cell door closes.

Major Linke: Come to the door.

Steven's handcuffs are removed through his cell's letterbox. The Narrator addresses the audience once more.

Narrator: In the closing months of 2000, another Texan fraudster made headlines when Governor George W. Bush stole the presidential election from Vice President Al Gore, and became America's 43rd President.

Steven: How could Americans be so stupid?

Narrator: A sentiment echoed throughout the world.

Steven: Thank God he'll only be a one-term president. Mark my words: America won't make the same mistake twice.

Narrator: Of course, America would go on to make the same mistake twice, but for now that's still four years away.

The Beautiful Woman enters from stage left carrying a card with the year '2001' written on it.

Narrator: Now, everyone knows what happened on September 11,

2001.

When the first plane hit New York's Twin Towers, we were listening to a local radio station when programming was interrupted for a breaking-news alert.

Like when Kennedy died and Pearl Harbor was attacked, everyone remembers where they were when they heard about 9/11. For Steven and me, it was easy. We were here. The same place we'd been for three and a half years.

The reaction in Gabriel Unit was the same as everywhere else in America. Inmates were outraged at what had transpired and hungry for revenge. It may surprise you to know that, despite being imprisoned and unable to vote, inmates don't necessarily hate the government that keeps them here, nor are they unpatriotic.

An Islamic inmate, who cheered and shouted Allahu Akbar when he heard about the 9/11 attacks, was beaten up by a group of prisoners and had to be sent to solitary for his own safety, pending transfer to another jail.

Something else happened on September 11, however. Something that went largely unnoticed by a shocked and grieving population: a prisoner escaped from Gabriel Unit!

Steven: Only for once it wasn't me.

Narrator: But it was someone we knew. The young man we'd befriended when we worked in classification. Chris, the kid who held for us the police radio and clothes we stole, had gone one better this time and actually escaped. Can you believe it? He climbed out of his cell through a ventilation shaft. How brilliant and old school is that? Of course, this was too good an opportunity to miss.

Steven (*typing a letter on his typewriter and reading it out loud*):

"Dear Warden Alvarado,"

"It has come to my attention that, despite your best efforts, you allowed one of your inmates to escape Gabriel Unit on the night of September 11, 2001."

"Doubtless, the blemishing of your otherwise perfect record will have caused you much heartbreak. Rest assured, it is nothing compared to how you'll feel when I eventually walk out of Gabriel Unit and into that wide, sweet abyss called freedom."

"Given the above event, shamelessly and remorselessly splashed across the prison, local and Texan press, I have two recommendations for you that I hope you will act upon swiftly."

"Firstly, might I venture the opinion that, had you not allocated quite so many man-hours to keeping yours-truly under lock and key, you might have had sufficient staffing elsewhere to have avoided the escape of September 11?"

"Secondly, according to my information, Lieutenant Ramsey was the duty guard at the building from which Chris Jeffries managed to escape. Might I humbly request that he be transferred immediately and put in charge of my building?"

"Your brother through Jesus Christ,"

"Steven Russell."

Narrator: Christmas was celebrated with a meal of ham, roast potatoes, carrots, peas, green beans and stuffing followed by chocolate cake. Or, for those who required it, the Kosher and Halal alternative of roast potatoes, carrots, peas, green beans and stuffing followed by chocolate cake.

The Beautiful Woman enters from stage left carrying a card with the year '2002' written on it.

Narrator: 2002 was a marked improvement on 2001. January brought the news that PhyCor, the parent company of NAMM, the medical company we 'borrowed' $800,000 from, had gone bankrupt.

Now, you might think the money we took from them contributed to their downfall, but you would be wrong.

As a matter of fact, 1996, the year PhyCor's CEO hired us to take charge of NAMM's finances, turned out to be their most profitable year ever. That year the group reported a record profit of $36.4m. It was only after we left that things slowly turned to shit.

In the years that followed, overexpansion, the rising cost of healthcare and various personnel-related problems brought PhyCor to its knees. By the end of 1997 the group's profitability had fallen to just $3.2m a year. From there things only got worse.

In 1998 PhyCor recorded a loss of $111.4m and the year after that they lost a massive $445m. That's almost half a billion dollars! Gone.

Was PhyCor badly run? I'll let you be the judge of that, but let me share a few more facts for your consideration.

First of all, they hired me as the Chief Financial Officer of NAMM, despite the fact I was a convicted felon that had falsified every qualification on my resume.

Secondly, they let me run NAMM's finance department for almost five months even though I had no idea what I was doing.

Thirdly, they only noticed the $800,000 I stole from them because the bank the company used happened to be the same one I had my own personal account with, and it was the bank that pointed the transfers out to them.

When PhyCor went bankrupt, its stockholders lost everything. In its bankruptcy filing, the company listed just $28.9m in assets compared to more than $338m of debt. As such, PhyCor's creditors lost more than $300m of their money as well.

When PhyCor came out of bankruptcy in July 2002, its name had changed to Aveta Health Inc. and all traces and links to the previous company were gone.

Despite losing more than $500m of other people's money, no criminal charges were ever brought against PhyCor's former management. Why? Because they lost money the legal way. They worked the system, unintentionally or otherwise. Do you think they paid back their bonuses and salaries to the people whose money they lost? Of course they didn't.

And here's a thought for you: I was given 45 years for stealing $800,000. If PhyCor's board and management were given prison time in the same ratio for the money they lost, they'd currently be serving sentences of more than 28,000 years.

Back to more important matters, 2002 was also the year we finished our work with Steve McVicker and received important news from Phillip.

Major Linke throws two items of mail through the letterbox of Steven's cell.

Major Linke: Mail call!

Steven lies motionless on his bunk.

Narrator: Aren't you going to get that?

Steven: I'll get it in a minute.

Narrator (*to Steven*): No, really you need to pick those up and read them.

Steven: I'm taking a nap. I'll get them later.

Narrator: No. I say, "2002 was also the year we finished our work with Steve McVicker and received important news from Phillip," and then you open the two letters that land on the floor. One's from McVicker and the other one's from Phillip.

Steven: I'll do it later.

Narrator: That's not how it's meant to happen!

The Narrator walks over and picks up the letters and holds them out for Steven to take. Steven ignore him.

Steven: Just put them over there, would you?

Narrator: No, you have to read them.

Steven: Bite me.

Major Linke enters from stage left, taking the number of cast members on stage to three.

Major Linke: Open the goddamned letters, Steven! You're holding up the interval.

Steven: You as well? Would you both just leave me alone?

Narrator: Oh, for goodness sake!

The Beautiful Woman enters from stage right, taking the number of cast members on stage to four.

Beautiful Women (*complaining*): Seriously Steven, just open the letters!

Steven: You too? You're not even meant to have lines.

Warden Alvarado appears from stage left taking the number on stage to five.

Warden: Steven, would you just read the letters? We're all waiting.

Steven: You?!!! You can't be here! Stay out of this. Anyway, if the letters have made their way here you should have read them already.

Warden: One of my underlings read them. They haven't briefed me yet. Just open them! (*Pointing*) There's a lady in the second row who looks like she needs to use the restroom.

Steven (*shouting*): Fine! Alright!

He takes both letters from the Narrator.

Narrator: Thank you.

Steven: Anything for some peace and quiet.

Beautiful Woman: Which one are you opening first?

Steven: It's the one from Phillip.

Warden: And what does it say?

Steven: He says… He says he's being paroled in November.

Warden: Bullshit! Give me that.

The Warden walks into Steven's cell, takes the letter from him and begins reading it.

Beautiful Woman: Well, that's great news!

Narrator: It's good news for us. It's bad news for the Warden because technically that means Phillip can come and visit us.

Warden (*fuming*): I won't allow it!

Major Linke (*to the Warden*): Can you do that?

Steven: Of course he can't.

Beautiful Women: What does the other letter say, Steven?

Steven (*opening the second letter*): Well, we know it's from Steve McVicker.

"Dear Steven,"

"Great news! Miramax Books have expressed an interest in our book and have penciled in a publication date of July 2003."

Warden: That's not possible!

Narrator: That's awesome!!

Steven: There's more...

"Additionally, some independent film-makers have expressed an interest in turning the book into a motion picture."

Everyone except Warden Alvarado expresses excitement at this.

Warden (*cursing*): Goddamn it!

Steven: "To that end, two Hollywood scriptwriters have asked me if they could come and see you. Their names are John Requa and Glenn Ficarra."

Narrator (*jumping in the air*): Jackpot!

Major Linke: That's amazing!

Warden (*chastising him*): Major!

Major Linke: Sorry, Warden. I mean, (*shaking his fist*) damn you Russell!

Beautiful Woman: You're going to be in a movie?

Steven (*to the Narrator*): McVicker says I should treat their visit like an audition. If they like me, these are the guys that will be writing the film's script.

Narrator: When are they planning on coming?

Steven: They want to fly to Texas early next year.

Warden (*angrily*): Shit.

Narrator: Yippee! Well, roll on 2003.

Blackout. The CURTAIN falls.

ACT TWO

SCENE ONE

The CURTAIN rises revealing the same stage general arrangement as Act One.

Steven and the Narrator are lying center stage on two sun loungers, bathed in red and yellow light. Hawaiian music is playing. Steven lies on the lounger to the right while the Narrator sits on the lounger to the left. Each of them has a parasol in one hand and a cocktail in the other. Both are wearing straw sun hats and sunglasses.

Narrator (*cheerily*):   Well, hello again! Glad you could join us. It's 2003 and Steven and I are … (*he looks around*) Actually, I have no idea where we are. Steven, where are we?

Steven (*casually*): It looks like Santa Monica to me.

Narrator (*confused*): California?

Steven: Is there another?

Narrator (*taking off his sunglasses*): Steven, that's not possible. If this is the future and we've been paroled then we'd have to stay in Texas under the terms of our parole.

Steven: Oh. (*Smiling and relaxing*) Well, then we're on Port Aransas

Beach, Nueces County, Texas.

Narrator: Of course, we are. (*To the audience*) We're celebrities now. Some people from Hollywood are flying in to make a motion picture about lil' ol' me.

Steven: Lil' ol' us!

Narrator: Yes. Tell me, Steven... (*He sips his drink*) ... What kinds of people do they make films about?

Steven: Kings and emperors usually. Presidents. Those kinds of people.

Narrator: Rock stars as well, don't forget. Famous, important, historical figures. (*He sips his drink*) They like to make biopics about them, don't they?

Steven: Inventors too... like Thomas Edison and Henry Ford.

Narrator: Oh and astronauts, of course. Brave, fearless men flying to the moon.

Steven: Murderers...

Narrator: Well, yes... But also composers, industrialists....

Steven: Warmongers.

Narrator: And war heroes. And also great painters, poets and writers...

Steven: And perverts.

Narrator (*shouting*): Steven! You're ruining my 'us time.' (*Calmly*) My point is they don't just make films about anyone, do they? They make films about special people and that there makes us special.

Steven: Whatever.

Narrator (*excitedly*): We're like Bonnie and Clyde rolled into one.

Steven: I think you've had a little bit too much to drink.

Narrator: Or Sweeney Todd and Mrs Lovett.

Steven: Fine. You're Mrs Lovett.

The Narrator puts his sunglasses back on.

Narrator (*like a Southern lady*): Now, Steven, my piña colada is empty! Would you be a darling and refill my glass?

Steven: Refill it yourself. This is my daydream.

Narrator: It is not! I'm just as asleep as you are.

Steven: No, you're not.

Narrator: I am, too. I'm in a thoroughly relaxed and deep sleep.

Steven: Well, you can't be. People only dream when they're in shallow sleep.

Narrator: Well then, I'm in a thoroughly relaxed and shallow sleep.

Steven (*boasting*): I'm in a coma.

Narrator: You are not!

Steven: I am too. How would you know if I'm in a coma or not?

Narrator: Well, because then we'd both be in a coma. I think I'd know if I was in coma.

Steven: I wish you were in a coma.

Narrator: What time are they arriving?

Steven: We're in prison, numbnuts. It's not like they made an appointment. Visiting hours are from 10 a.m. to 4 p.m. They can turn up any time they like.

Narrator: They said they'd be here after lunch though, didn't they?

Steven: Yes, but they don't know the local area. More than likely they'll have underestimated how long it takes to get here.

Narrator: But they flew in last night, right?

Steven: That was the plan.

Narrator: I hate all this uncertainty! I don't even know if I have time to roll over and tan my back. As celebrities, I think we deserve better treatment than this.

Steven: We're still in prison, you moron! When they're here, a guard will come to fetch us. We've done this a thousand times before.

Narrator: Are you nervous? I'm nervous. McVicker said we should treat this like an audition. We need to impress them.

Steven: Nope.

Narrator: We don't need to impress them?

Steven: No, I'm not nervous.

Narrator: Not even a little bit?

Steven: Not even a little bit.

Narrator: Not even a little, iddy, biddy bit?

Steven: Not even that.

Narrator: Well, why not?

Steven: Because they already know our life story. If they weren't already impressed they wouldn't have got on a plane and come out here, would they?

Narrator: They're the real deal, you know?

Steven: I would hope they are.

Narrator: I did some research on the last film they did. Want me to tell you?

Steven: How did you manage to research their last film?

Narrator: Never you mind. Do you want to know what I found out?

Steven: Go on.

Narrator: It was called *Cats and Dogs*.

Steven: Was it a gritty take on the subtle differences between the sexes, set in the modern dating scene?

Narrator: No, it was a film about… cats and dogs.

Steven: Was it?

Narrator: It was a comedy.

Steven: A comedy?

Narrator: You know, funny ha-ha.

Steven: Do they think we're funny ha-ha?

Narrator: I think we might be. To an outsider.

Steven: Who was in it? Anyone famous like … Lassie? Or that white cat from the James Bond films?

Narrator: There were lots of famous people in it, actually. Tobey Maguire for one.

Steven: Who's he?

Narrator: The new Spiderman.

Steven: Really? Who else?

Narrator: Jeff Goldblum. He was that scientist who became a fly in... *The Fly*.

Steven: Well, they must have gotten along well together.

Narrator: Sean Hayes was in it too.

Steven: Now he's funny.

Narrator: And Charlton Heston.

Steven: Isn't he dead?

Narrator: What year is it?

Steven: 2003.

Narrator: Then, no. Not yet.

Steven: Anyone else?

Narrator: Alec Baldwin.

Steven: Now, I always say, if you're going to have a successful film, you have to have a Baldwin in it. Was it successful?

Narrator: It cost $60 million to make and grossed more than $200 million.

Steven: Wow.

Narrator: I know, right? These guys are pretty good. Are you nervous now?

Steven: Nope.

Narrator: Why not?

Steven: Because we are a damned sight more interesting than dogs licking their nuts and chasing cats. Or whatever that film was about.

Major Linke (*from outside the cell door*): Come to the door! You got a visitor.

Steven (*taking one last sip from his drink*): That's my cue. Here, you'd better take these.

Steven hands the narrator his paraphernalia.

Narrator: What? I'm coming with you. I want to see this.

Steven backs up to his cell door and has his hands handcuffed behind his back. The lights go out in Steven's cell. Stagehands remove the two sun loungers.

ACT TWO

SCENE TWO

The lights come on in the visitors' area. Steven is led through the blue bar door by Major Linke and is seated on his side of the Plexiglas. The Narrator hovers around him.

John Requa and Glenn Ficarra enter the visitors' area from stage left and take a seat on their side of the divide. Steven picks up a phone receiver and John and Glenn do the same.

Steven: Well, you guys must be John and Glenn. I'm Steven Russell.

John: Hi Steven, I'm John Requa.

Glenn: Which makes me Glenn Ficarra.

John: It's such a pleasure to finally meet you in person, having read so much about you.

Narrator (*to Steven*): Do you think they're a couple?

Steven: Well it's awfully nice to meet the two of you.

John: Thanks for putting us on your visitors' list.

Narrator (*to Steven*): Which one of them do you think is the top?

Steven: You're more than welcome.

Glenn (*laughing*): So, are we your cousins today?

Narrator (*whispering and pointing to Glenn*): I think he's the bottom.

Steven: Something like that. Arranging an official media visit seems to be pretty much impossible these days.

John: They're that bad here?

Steven: You don't know the half of it. They read all my mail, they can censor it if they see fit. They only stopped reading my legal mail after I threatened to sue them. Legal correspondence is meant to be private and confidential. The warden here is under the impression that I might escape at any time, so he errs on the side of overcautious most of the time. Even if it's illegal.

Glenn: That must have made writing the book very difficult.

Steven: It was. It took a lot of patience and time, but we managed it in the end. I'll be honest and say that McVicker isn't the greatest writer in the world, too many years writing copy I think, but he did a good job.

John: Is there anything about the book you're unhappy with?

Steven: Not really. Maybe the title.

John: *I Love You Phillip Morris?*

Steven: McVicker was keen to include Phillip's name in the title, for recognition purposes. What with it being the same as the tobacco company and all. I'm sure you guys will use a different title for the film, right?

Glenn: Actually, we love the title.

Narrator (*to Steven*): I have a bad feeling about this.

Steven: You do?

Glenn: Yeah. Because as crazy as the action gets, as far-out as the scams and the prison breaks go, (*he turns to John momentarily*) what we love about it is, at its core, yours is a good old-fashioned love story.

Narrator: Bullshit!

Steven (*nodding*): Yes. Yes, it is.

Narrator (*shouting*): No, it isn't. Come on guys. Don't do this to me!

Glenn: Of course, the studio has some reservations.

Steven: Do they? So they might not buy the movie rights after all?

John: Oh, they've already bought the rights. What we're working on now is the script. Then after the script comes the funding. Miramax have right of first refusal on a finalized proposal, but we kind of get the feeling they're not sold on one small detail.

Steven: What's that?

Glenn: Let's just say they would prefer it if Phillip was actually called Philippa.

Narrator (*to Steven*): I told you.

Steven: Ah.

John: We don't agree. We'd rather keep the film as true to the original story as possible. Obviously we'll need to simplify some of the details to make it audience-friendly, but rewriting it as a love story between a man and a woman seems to us, a step too far.

Narrator (*referring to John and Glenn*): They are so gay. Look at them.

Gay clothes, gay shoes. Gay faces.

Steven (*ignoring the Narrator*): Is the studio concerned the gay angle might affect the film's economics?

John: You know, it's 2003. There are still an awful lot of Americans, as well as others around the world, who won't go and see what they perceive as a gay film.

Glenn: Although we won't be making a gay film. We want to make a good film about an extraordinary man and the things he did for love. Namely, escape prison four times, impersonate a CFO and steal a million dollars.

John: We think we can tell your story in an interesting way as well. Glenn and I have talked about it. We like the idea of making a film about a conman and making the audience his last victim.

Steven: In what way would the audience be my last victim?

Glenn: We'll serially misdirect them. We'll start off showing you, your wife and daughter and then, only after five or ten minutes, will we reveal you're gay.

John: We'll use your internal voice to narrate the film too; so, when you finally pull your AIDS escape from the hospice, we can fool the audience into thinking you're actually dead.

Steven: My internal voice, eh?

Narrator: Are they talking about me? Am I going to be in the movie?

Steven: That all sounds like clever stuff.

Glenn: But at its heart it's still *Don Quixote*.

John: By which he means it's still a love story. Phillip is obviously Dulcinea.

Narrator: What the fuck are they talking about?

Glenn: Have you read the new translation of *Don Quixote*, Steven?

Steven: Oh, yes.

Narrator: You liar.

John: We'd both just finished it when Andrew Lazar and Far Shariat, two producers, showed us the proposal for your book.

Glenn: What was your reason for writing the book, by the way? What was your motivation?

Steven: My reason? (*He pauses*) There are a few answers to that question. First of all, aside from the movie nights, the seaside excursions, the swimming pool and solarium... there's not a whole heap of stuff to do when you're in solitary. Keeping my brain active is how I've been able to stay sane.

Narrator: Or sane-ish, depending on your point of view.

Steven: You see, your brain is like every other muscle in your body. If you don't use it, you lose it. Also, I wanted to set the record straight. I've never been charged with two of the four escapes I managed, and no one had ever connected the dots and realized that all my escapes took place on Friday the 13th. When you're locked up like I am, surrounded by other cons, reputation counts for a lot. I want to make sure I'm given full credit for what I've achieved over the years.

John: Won't spelling out everything you did create more trouble for yourself?

Steven: Not at all. What can they do to me now? As it is I'm not likely to ever make it out of here. So, in that sense there's nothing I can lose.

Glenn: Won't it mean you can never escape again?

Steven: Maybe. There are two ways of looking at it. On the one hand, I'm getting older and the security they have around me now is tighter than ever. So maybe I'll never escape again. On the other hand, how much of a slap in the face would it be to share with the world every detail of my previous escapes, including the people who run this prison, and still be able to walk out of here? So who knows, maybe I'll see you at the premiere of your film.

John: We obviously have access to McVicker's manuscript, so we don't need to ask you too many detailed questions. Let me ask you a more general question though: how were you able to do the things you did?

Steven: Confidence and common sense. That and the fact that I look like an average Joe. People just don't seem to suspect me. So whether I'm impersonating a judge, a federal agent or a company bigwig, they assume that's exactly who I am.

I do my homework, of course. You have to remember that a man or a woman, no different from you or me, does every job in the world. So if I studied and worked hard, I too could be a judge or a federal agent. I could be a chief financial officer. The only reason I'm not is because I don't want to be. I don't want to put in the time to make that happen. But would I speak any differently if I were? No. Maybe I'd dress slightly differently, but then again maybe not.

So, what's stopping me from being any of those people now? Nothing. Everyone can act. Everybody tells lies, little ones or otherwise. To their co-workers or their friends. Sometimes people even lie to themselves. I'm just less inhibited in how I use that skill and less afraid of the repercussions for doing so.

He turns directly to John.

You must have lied, John? Maybe to impress a date?

He turns to Glenn.

Glenn, you must have said something at one time, whether in an interview or at a party, that stretched the truth a little? When you guys write, you pretend to know what the characters you're writing for would say. You make educated guesses. You put yourself in their position and think about what you would do. How you would feel. Movies really are one big con aren't they? For ninety minutes or longer your job is to convince us that everything happening on the screen is real. And if you're good at what you do, we believe you.

Glenn: Why was your love for Phillip so intense?

Steven: My love for Phillip is…

Narrator: Was.

Steven: … was intense for a number of reasons. First of all I tend to obsess about things. I was only diagnosed with obsessive-compulsive disorder last year, so now I can put a name to it. But I can tell you that I've always had it. So that has something to do with it.

Phillip and I met in prison, of course, which is not the healthiest of places to start or conduct a relationship. And we met not long after my former partner, Jimmy, died. With hindsight, I'm not sure I was fully over Jimmy's death when Phillip and I started up. In those final months with Jimmy, I had to fight to get him the care he needed. I'm not very good at taking 'no' for an answer when it comes to someone I love and, in those last months with Jimmy, there was an awful lot of 'no'.

Glenn: When did you first realize you were gay?

Narrator: Probably about the same time that you did, Glenn.

Steven: Oh, I've always known. When I married my now ex-wife though, I thought I could override it. I thought we could be together and raise a family just like everybody else. It was only later that I realized pretending everything was OK wasn't fair on her, our daughter or me.

Narrator: Ask them what it was like working with Jeff Goldblum.

Steven (*to the narrator*): No.

John: It must have been a very confusing time for you.

Steven: Being married to a woman, or the last forty-six years?

They all laugh, except the Narrator.

Narrator: Ask them if Sean Hayes' eyes are as blue and sparkly in real life as they are on television.

John: I'm just throwing names out here, Steven, but how would you feel about Woody Harrelson playing you?

Steven: Why? Is Brad Pitt busy?

They all laugh again, except for the Narrator.

Narrator (*to Steven*): Quit ignoring me. I'm just trying to have a little fun.

Steven (*to the Narrator*): Will you shut the fuck up?

Narrator: Fine. Have it your way. Ask them if Charlton Heston had any flu-like symptoms the last time they saw him!

The Narrator storms off back to Steven's cell, whereupon the lights come back on there. He lies down on the bed.

Steven (*to the Narrator*): Would you stop being such a baby?

John: Steven? Woody Harrelson?

Steven (*focusing again*): I think he'd be great.

Glenn: We're talking to Gus Van Sant about directing, too. There's no guarantee he'll say yes, but it seems like the kind of project that would interest him.

Steven: Wasn't he the guy that did *Good Will Hunting?*

John: He got nominated for an Oscar for it, too.

Glenn: We're a long way off, of course, but just out of interest, would you be available for promotion? When the film comes out? If the studio arranged for journalists to come and see you here, like we have? Is there a limit to how many cousins you can have?

Steven: Not at all. I have a very big family. I'm happy to help in any way I can and, again, anything that keeps me busy keeps me sane and out of trouble.

John: I should warn you, Steven, not to expect this to be a quick process. We have a film coming out later this year that we need to focus on.

Steven: Really? What's it called?

Glenn: *Bad Santa*. It's another comedy, this time aimed at the Christmas market.

Steven: Who's in it?

John: Billy Bob Thornton.

Glenn: We're also working on a remake of *The Bad News Bears.*

Steven: Well, it sounds like you guys certainly have your hands full.

John: We're really excited about bringing your story to life. I just wanted you to know that these things take time.

Steven: Most things in life seem to. The good news is, for you at least, I'm not going anywhere.

Major Linke (*returning*): Time's up, Russell.

Steven (*standing up*): Come back and see me whenever you want.

Steven backs up to Major Linke to have his hands cuffed.

John (*standing up*): Thank you, Steven, we will. It's been great talking to you.

Glenn (*also standing up*): Thanks again for your time. It was great to meet you.

Steven: You're more than welcome.

The lights go out in the visitors' area. Glenn and John leave stage left. Steven is taken back to his cell by Major Linke.

ACT TWO

SCENE THREE

Steven is uncuffed through his cell door in the usual way. The Narrator is waiting for him.

Steven: Are you still sulking, you little fame-whore?

Narrator: You do know that when you call me names you're calling yourself the same, right?

Steven: Well, you missed them telling us that Gus Van Sant might sign on to direct our film.

Narrator: Really? That's amazing. Didn't he do that film with Keanu Reeves and River Phoenix?

Steven: *My Own Private Idaho*!

Narrator: Now that was hot.

Steven: It was, wasn't it? I would say that things are most definitely looking up for us.

Narrator: Did they tell you which one of them is the top?

Steven: I'm not even sure they're gay. They're liberals, for sure. Gay-friendly, yes. But actually gay? I don't know.

Narrator: You can never really tell with creative types can you?

Steven: Well, whatever they are, they're good at what they do, they like us, and they like our story. I have a feeling that this is going to be a very good year.

The lights go down in the cell. The Narrator stands up from the bunk and walks down to center stage where a spotlight falls on him.

Narrator: And it was a good year. In some ways. And in other ways it was kind of shitty. Our work with Steve McVicker had finished and Glenn and John weren't lying when they said they'd picked up the rights to turn it into a movie.

The book came out in June and while sales of *I Love You Phillip Morris* were initially modest, McVicker knew that they were bound to increase when, and if, a film of the same name was released.

The book itself was banned from Gabriel Unit and all other TDCJ facilities so, although we saw a final copy of the manuscript, we never managed to see a copy of the book we helped write.

One of the consequences of the book being out there was that almost every detail of my life was now public knowledge, including my sexuality, the fact I was adopted, as well as all the escapes and cons. And all in far greater detail than had ever been reported in newspapers or magazines.

Here in jail, no one gave a shit about my sexuality. However, they were impressed, and in some cases overjoyed, with how I made clowns of everyone in TDCJ. Alvarado may have hated it, but I cemented my reputation as Gabriel Unit's resident celebrity.

2003 was also the year that TDCJ decided to end the practice whereby inmates could write to other inmates through the prison postal system. But what had always existed alongside the postal system was the black-market kite system: a prisoner-operated system for inmates to pass messages to one another without vetting from the post room.

Kites were usually delivered at the same time as meals, during recreation, during janitorial services, maintenance, you name it. So all that happened as a result of the ban was an increase in the number of kites, none of which were read by the prison mailroom.

The change meant that contacting inmates at other TDCJ units became more difficult, and that meant Phillip was unable to contact us in the five months before he was released on parole. However, after he was paroled, in November 2003, there was nothing to stop him. He could even visit us if he wanted. Only he didn't.

The lights go back on in Steven's cell.

Major Linke: Mail call.

Major Linke posts a letter thought Steven's letterbox.

Narrator: It was only after he'd been released that we received a letter from him, the first time we'd heard from him in months…

Steven picks up the letter from the floor of his cell and reads it out loud.

Steven: "Dear Steven,"

"I wanted to write and thank you for the money you put aside for me, for when I got out of jail. I have some bad news though. Promise you won't get mad at me? Well, unfortunately it's all gone now. Things sure have gotten more expensive while I was in prison…"

Narrator: For whatever reason, call it a misplaced sense of responsibility after all the years we'd been together, we arranged for some money to be sent to Phillip. Legitimate money. To help him get back on his feet after being paroled.

Well, Phillip had spent it all. Although a lot of it doubtless went on alcohol, we were at pains to emphasize to him that money tends to run out when you have no income and make little or no effort to get a job.

Steven (*reading*): "I've moved in with a preacher and his wife from the local Assembly of God" Jesus Christ! "They're nice people, but I have to admit I've hit rock bottom. I was hoping you could see it in your heart to send me some more money. For old times' sake. Because the way I see it, you owe me."

Narrator: Now that was a lie. Steven and I lied through our teeth to try and get Phillip off the NAMM charge even though, in truth, he was as guilty as we were. We'd been more than generous. Much more. Then, as if to encourage us to be sympathetic towards him, Phillip said something that did quite the opposite.

Steven: "See, the thing is, Steven, I don't know how to tell you this, but I found out recently I'm HIV-positive. I didn't want to tell you about it before, which is probably the reason I didn't write you as often as maybe I should have this past year. The truth is, three other inmates at Hughes Unit sexually assaulted me. Long term, I've been told I should be eligible for Social Security disability, not least because the prison authorities allowed it to happen, but in the meantime I was wondering if you could sub me for a while. We can call it a loan if you like and I could pay you back?"

Narrator: Now, if you believe that, you'll believe anything. (*Pause*) Phillip's letter troubled us. Mainly because I couldn't believe he was the victim of a sexual assault while in prison. Had he been, we would have heard about it from other inmates or from the prison officials. There would have been some noise because of Phillip's and our high-profile status.

TDCJ has a zero-tolerance policy towards sexual misbehavior. If anyone complains of sexual assault, the victim is removed from general population and placed in administrative lockdown while members of the Office of the Inspector General investigate the incident. Where was Phillip's investigation?

If it wasn't true, why was he feeding me this story? Had he been having an affair with another inmate at Hughes Unit? It was possible. And if he was, why wasn't he asking him for money rather than me? I didn't know who or what to believe, but I thought I smelled a rat.

In the past I would have done anything for Phillip. Anything. All he had to do was ask. Now I found myself looking back at everything we'd been through and re-evaluating everything he'd said. The trust was gone. Our relationship had always had a slight edge to it. I didn't always tell him the truth, so I'm sure that worked both ways, but up until then I'd always given him the benefit of the doubt. Would I ever be able to do that again?

Steven (*shaking his head*): No.

Narrator: No. Although just because I thought I was seeing Phillip in a new light doesn't mean that the drama associated with him ended. The following year, Warden Alvarado decided to punish me by taking Phillip's name back off my visitors' list.

Why was he punishing me? Well, because of a letter I'd sent to the Media Relations Officer of Gabriel Unit.

ACT TWO

SCENE FOUR

The lights go on in Warden Alvarado's office. Warden Alvarado is sitting at his desk. Gabriel Unit's Media Relations Officer is seated opposite him.

Media Relations Officer: I've received a letter from Steven Russell.

Warden: Full of wisecracks, no doubt?

Media Relations Officer: This is something we need to take seriously.

Warden: I'll be the judge of that. What did he say?

Media Relations Officer: It's not just what he said, it's what he sent to me. The letter he wrote to me included a piece of hacksaw blade and an improvised knife.

Warden (*not believing his ears*): He knowingly sent you contraband?

Media Relations Officer: In the letter he complains that because he is moved from cell to cell so often, he frequently finds himself in cells containing illegal items. He claims the cell's former occupants never have sufficient time to collect their contraband before being moved out to make way for him.

He says that if his cells are not thoroughly cleaned and checked before he moves in, the next time he finds a blade or any other item of contraband, he's sending it straight to *The Houston Journal*'s news desk.

Warden: That cannot be allowed to happen.

Media Relations Officer: Then you'll issue an appropriate order to your staff directing them to sweep the cells first?

Warden (*shaking his head*): That's not what I meant. I'm understaffed as it is. No, we'll simply instruct the post room to vet all and any mail he sends to media organizations in addition to all of his personal mail.

Media Relations Officer: Sir, you're aware that's against state law?

Warden: I'm afraid I didn't hear you properly. Would you care to repeat that?

Media Relations Officer: I think you heard me perfectly.

Warden: I'm not having that little shit dictate what our policies will be in dealing with him.

Media Relations Officer: Fine, but if I'm ever asked I will deny all knowledge of this conversation. And you can give the mailroom the order yourself.

Warden: Fine. I would ask you to do one thing for me though. Pop by administration on your way back to your office and have them remove Phillip Morris from Russell's visitors' list.

Media Relations Officer: Sir?

Warden: He has to understand who's in charge here. And it's not him, do you understand? Have Morris taken off.

Media Relations Officer: Yes, sir.

The Media Relations Officer leaves Warden Alvarado's office as all the lights there go out.

ACT TWO

SCENE FIVE

A spotlight comes on the Narrator, who stands center-stage addressing the audience.

Narrator: By now Phillip was a free man, and while I never expected he would actually come and visit me at Gabriel Unit, I knew that having him on my visitors' list scared the hell out of Alvarado. So, once again I turned to State Representative Terri Hodge to pull Alvarado back in line. She took the matter right to the top of TDCJ and, though it took a few months, Phillip was eventually put back on my visitors' list.

Glenn and John continued to make waves in Hollywood. Their film, *Bad Santa*, starring Billy Bob Thornton, grossed more than $75 million, while the other film they mentioned, *Bad News Bears*, also starring Thornton, grossed $35 million.

With the film version of *I Love You Phillip Morris* still in development, I spent my time keeping Warden Alvarado on his toes. Did you know that between the beginning of 2004 and the end of 2006 there were a total of five Friday the 13ths?

The lights go on in Steven's Russell's cell. Major Linke and Lt. Herrera are crouched down outside the sliding door to Steven's cell. The Narrator sits on the floor of Steven's cell reading Time Magazine.

Steven (*sitting on his bunk reading the Wall Street Journal*): I know you're out there.

Silence.

Steven and the Narrator look at each other and shake their heads.

Steven (*after a while*): I can hear you breathing.

Major Linke (*to Lt. Herrera*): I said you were breathing too loudly!

Lt. Herrera: It's the chemicals they use to clean their cells. It gets in the back of my throat.

Steven: Do you guys really think I would be dumb enough to try and escape on a Friday the 13th again?

Major Linke (*talking to Steven*): Look Russell, we're just following orders, OK? We know you know we're here. We know it's stupid. But we were told to sit outside of your cell all day today in case you try and make a run for it.

Steven: You guys have been out there all morning? Can I get either of you a coffee?

Lt. Herrera: Cream and two sugars, please.

Major Linke: He is not allowed to make you coffee! What would the Warden say?

Lt. Herrera (*to Major Linke*): Sorry. (*To Steven*) I mean, no, thank you.

Steven (*turning the page of his newspaper*): Do you guys have cushions to sit on?

Lt. Herrera: No.

Steven: Well your asses must be number than Alvarado's brain.

Lt. Herrera: Mine is.

Major Linke: Lieutenant!

They all sit in silence for a few seconds.

Lt. Herrera: Hey, Steven?

Steven (*turning another page of his newspaper*): Yes?

Lt. Herrera: I heard something about your film the other day. My wife read about it in a magazine. One of the glossy ones you see near the registers. It said Jim Carrey was going to play you.

Steven (*Surprised*): Really? Jim Carrey? (*He turns to the Narrator*) Is that true?

Narrator: It's true, alright.

Steven (*putting his newspaper down*): Wasn't he in *The Truman Show*?

Narrator: Yep. Which grossed more than $260 million and won him the Golden Globe for Best Actor.

Lt. Herrera: He was in *The Mask* too!

Narrator (*still not looking up*): Which grossed more than $350 million. Carrey also won another Golden Globe for his portrayal of Andy Kaufman in *Man on The Moon* and starred as The Grinch in *How The Grinch Stole Christmas*, Bruce in *Bruce Almighty*, and Ace Ventura in *Ace Ventura: Pet Detective* and its sequel.

Major Linke: He played The Riddler in that *Batman* movie too.

Narrator (*still not looking up*): Altogether, the films he has starred in have grossed more than $2.4 billion.

Steven (*standing up*): Holy shit!

Narrator (*finally looking up from his magazine*): I guess Woody Harrelson was busy?

Steven (*enthusiastically*): And a good thing, too.

Lt. Herrera: Hey Steven, some British guy is going to play Phillip.

Steven walks over to his cell door and speaks through it.

Steven: Which one?

Lt. Herrera: I forget his name.

Steven: Have I heard of him?

Lt. Herrera: He was in that *Star Wars* film.

Steven: Alec Guinness?

Narrator: He's dead.

Steven: Harrison Ford?

Narrator: Since when was Harrison Ford British?

Lt. Herrera: He's in the new films.

Steven: Liam Neeson? (*He turns to the Narrator*) Is he British?

Narrator: Irish.

Steven: Isn't that part of Britain?

Narrator: Not since 1922.

Lt. Herrera: He's the one from *Moulin Rouge*.

Steven: Everyone was in *Moulin Rouge.*

Narrator: Ask him if he means Ewan McGregor.

Steven (*to Lt. Herrera*): Do you mean Ewan McGregor? The guy from *Trainspotting?*

Lt. Herrera: Yeah, that's him! He's the one playing Phillip.

Steven: That's awesome news too. He's won Oscars, right?

Narrator: No.

Steven: But he's British. They always win.

Narrator: That may be so, but I'm afraid Ewan is, currently, Oscar-less.

Steven: Bummer. Poor Phillip. Jim Carrey, eh? And to think that Frank Abagnale had to settle for Leonardo DiCaprio.

Narrator: Right. And Buster Edwards had to settle for Phil Collins.

Steven: And he's not even an actor!

Narrator: Exactly.

Steven pauses for a moment.

Steven: But I look nothing like Jim Carrey. I look more like Woody Harrelson, which I suppose is why John and Glenn suggested him when they were here. I suppose Ewan McGregor looks a bit like Phillip, but Jim Carrey? Are they going to shave his head?

Narrator: Steven. Have you seen a picture of Frank Abagnale?

Steven: No. But I'm guessing he looks a lot like Leonardo DiCaprio.

Narrator: Well, he doesn't. That's why DiCaprio and Carrey are actors, not impressionists.

Steven: So, this is really happening? I mean, you know, right? It's really going to happen?

Narrator: Yes. It's really going to happen.

Lt. Herrera: Steven?

Steven: Yes?

Lt. Herrera: Who are you talking to?

Steven pauses again.

Steven (*innocently*): No one.

Lt. Herrera: Is someone in there with you?

Steven: Did you see anyone come in?

Lt. Herrera: No.

Steven: Then I'm the only one in here.

Lt. Herrera: OK. Just checking!

Steven (*happily*): Happy Friday the 13th.

Lt. Herrera (*just as happily*): You too.

The lights go out in Steven's cell.

ACT TWO

SCENE SIX

The lights go on in Warden Alvarado's office. The Warden is sitting at his desk looking at a piece of paper. Major Linke is standing to attention in front of him.

Warden: And you found this where, exactly?

Major Linke: We intercepted it on a meal tray being taken to Steven Russell.

Warden (*looking at the piece of paper*): Did you now? Have you tried to crack it?

Major Linke: Sir, I thought we'd have Russell decode it for us himself. I'm having him brought here right now.

Warden: Coming here?

Major Linke: Yes, sir. I thought you'd want to confront him.

Warden: Of course I do. Though I have to admit that generally the less I see of that man the better.

Major Linke: I've photocopied the kite, sir, just in case he tries to destroy it.

Warden: And how do we imagine he would do that?

Major Linke: He might swallow it, sir.

Warden: Good thinking, Major. If only all your colleagues were as conscientious as you are.

Major Linke: Thank you, sir.

The Warden's office door opens and in comes Steven, handcuffed and accompanied by Lt. Herrera. The Narrator appears also, having walked directly over from Steven's cell.

Warden (*acknowledging the prisoner*): Russell.

Steven: Warden. Always a pleasure.

Steven extends his hand to shake the Warden's, but the Warden does not extend his own.

Warden: I wish I could say the same.

Steven: Oh Warden, you hurt me with your words. I always thought you enjoyed our little chats.

Warden: Tell me, Russell, you do know it's an offense here at Gabriel Unit to communicate with other inmates in code, don't you?

Steven: Yes, Warden, I do.

Warden: Well, with that established then, would you mind telling me what this is?

Walden Alvarado hands Steven the kite.

Steven (*taking the kite and examining it*): It looks to me like a kite written in code.

Warden: That's exactly what it is, Russell and it was being sent to you.

Steven: And?

Warden: 'And?' That's your response?

Steven: If you tell me what you'd like me to say instead I'll gladly oblige.

Warden: I'll tell you what I want you to say. I want to know who it's from and what it says.

Steven: Ah, well, there I can't help you I'm afraid.

Warden: You can and you will, Russell.

Steven: Just let me check I've got his right. You're asking me who the encrypted message is from and what it says, right?

Warden (*losing patience*): Yes, Russell, that's exactly what I'm asking.

Steven: But… it's encrypted.

Warden: Yes, I know.

Steven: That means it's written in code.

Warden: I'm well aware of that.

Steven: So unless you have the key to decipher it, I can't help you.

Warden: You know the key, Russell.

Steven: Do I? Did you find it in my cell? Because if you did please return it. Actually come to think of it you'd better not. They frown on pieces of paper here when they have codes written on them.

Warden: It's in your head, Russell. We both know that. You know very well how this game works.

Steven: Warden, are you a mind reader now as well as the best warden in Texas?

Warden: I am slowly losing my patience.

Steven: It sounds like you almost lost it just then.

Warden: I want you to decode it for me and I want you to do it now.

Steven: Are you sure it's coded?

Warden: I'm very sure.

Steven: What if it's in Russian?

Warden: Is it in Russian?

Steven: How should I know? I don't speak Russian.

Warden: Then I'm guessing it's not in Russian, because whoever sent the kite to you wanted you to be able to read it.

Steven: Where did it come from?

Warden (*shouting*): Does it matter?

Steven: It's crucial.

Warden: It was found underneath the bun of your hamburger this evening.

Steven: The bun-half on top of the burger or between the burger and the lower bun-half?

Warden: Major?

Major Linke: Between the top bun-half and the burger, sir.

Steven: And today is a Tuesday, right?

Warden (*his patience wearing thin*): That's correct.

Steven: And who was on meal duty tonight for ad seg?

The Warden looks at Major Linke, prompting him to answer.

Major Linke: Ramirez.

Steven (*smiling*): Then I have all the information I need.

Warden: You're telling me that translating the code depends on the day of the week, whether the message was above or below the burger, and who delivered it?

Steven: Of course.

Narrator (*laughing to himself*): He can't believe that? You're going to give this guy a heart attack.

Warden: So what does it say?

Steven: Well, if Ramirez was the messenger then I'm guessing it comes from someone in the Mexican Mafia.

Warden: What... does it say?

Steven: I'll spell it out for you. Give me a second. Can someone write this down?

Warden (*to Major Linke*): Write it down.

Steven: Are you ready?

Major Linke (*picking up a pen and paper from the Warden's desk*): Ready.

Steven: The first letter is a 'W'. The second an 'E'. The third is an 'L'.

The fourth is an 'O'. The fifth… (*Pause*) is a 'W'… no sorry, a 'V' … then an 'E', a 'J', an 'I', an 'M', a 'C'… (*Pause*) an 'A', an 'R', another 'R', an 'E', and lastly a 'Y'.

The Narrator starts laughing.

Major Linke: That's not a message, that's just a load of jumbled up letters.

Steven: You have to break the letters up into words, dumbass. Specifically four words.

Warden: Give it here! (*He grabs the notes from Major Linke*) Four words, you say. So the message is: "We… (*Pause*) Love… (*Pause. He looks at Steven*) Jim Carrey"?

Steven: Exactly.

Warden (*annoyed*): Jim Carrey?

Steven: The Mexicans love him! I think because so much of what he does is physical comedy.

Warden: Don't fuck with me, Russell.

Steven: That's what it says! You know I get on well with the leaders of the Mexican Mafia in here. I mean, come on, it's either be friends with them or the Aryan Brotherhood of Texas, and obviously I prefer my taco-bearing amigos to those guys.

Warden (*wearily*): So now I have to have all the Mexican gang members removed from administrative segregation?

Steven: I'd rather you didn't. They've been a great help to me with what I'm planning. But if you're worried about them, there's another group of inmates you need to be more worried about. One that hasn't even appeared on your radar yet.

Warden: Enlighten me, Russell.

Steven: They're called the Pink Panthers.

Warden: Really? A gang of radical homosexuals?

Steven: We're just like the Tamil Tigers only much better dressed. We have gangbangs over in 4 Building every Friday night. Some of your guards pay us to watch.

Warden Alvarado slowly stands.

I'm their King Pin. The fairy godfather if you will...

Warden (*shouting*): Get out!

Major Linke moves over to Russell to escort him out.

Steven: It's all true! I swear it. But we're non-violent. We just corner inmates in their cells and criticize their clothes until they beg for mercy.

Warden: Out, I said! You too Linke! Quit wasting my time with this shit. I've got a prison to run for God's sake, I don't need this. I don't want it and I don't need it!

The lights go out in Warden Alvarado's office.

ACT TWO

SCENE SEVEN

A letter is posted through Steven's cell door. The Narrator arrives back in Steven's cell first, having taken his short cut. He picks up the letter from the floor. Steven and Major Linke arrive back at Steven's cell shortly afterwards. Major Linke uncuffs Steven through the letterbox of his cell.

Steven (*to Major Linke*): All I'm saying is, if you'd asked me to tell you what it said I would have told you. And we could have avoided you looking like an idiot in front of the warden.

Major Linke: You shouldn't wind him up like that. He'll take away your privileges again.

Steven: Trust me, none of them compare to the sight of his face when every blood vessel in his cheeks bursts simultaneously.

Major Linke: He's gonna crack one of these days, that's all I'm saying. You're asking for trouble.

Major Linke leaves stage left.

Narrator (*to Steven*): A letter arrived for you while you were gone. Looks like John Requa's writing.

Steven: Well open it. What's it about?

The Narrator opens the letter and reads its.

Narrator (*summarizing*): They've found funding for the film! Ten million dollars from Europe.

Steven: Shouldn't that be euro then?

Narrator (*reading*): He says they couldn't convince anyone here in America to fund it but that the Europeans were more than willing, solely on the back of Carrey's involvement.

Steven: You see. People love Jim Carrey. That's what I was saying to Warden Alvarado.

Narrator: Oh. (*Pause*) They go on to say that Gus Van Sant has dropped out to direct a biopic on Harvey Milk.

Steven: The gay politician?

Narrator: I can't think of any other.

Steven: So who's going to direct our film then?

Narrator: They're going to direct it themselves.

Steven: Really? I thought they were writers.

Narrator: They are.

Steven: Have they directed anything before?

Narrator: Do you want the long or the short answer?

Steven: The short one that won't leave me disappointed and with a strange sense of foreboding.

Narrator: The short answer is 'no'. This will be their directorial debut. John says it's a tremendous opportunity for them and will enable them to stay true to their vision for the film.

Steven: Should we be worried?

Narrator: Would it do us any good? I guess the people who stumped up the cash for the film aren't worried.

Steven: I suppose. Unless they don't speak English and couldn't read the contract properly.

Narrator: I guess Jim Carrey's not worried either.

Steven: Good point. And let's face it, how much direction could Jim Carrey possibly need? The man's a walking one-man show. He could direct himself if he needed to.

Narrator: And the cameramen are the ones with the real skills, right? I mean between them and the actors, they're the ones who pretty much decide what goes on.

Steven: So, really it's all good news then. The actors and funding are in place and we have a director on board who absolutely loves the script.

Narrator: Directors, plural. We now get two for the price of one.

Steven: I didn't think of it like that. Any word on when they might actually start filming?

Narrator: Early 2008. John also asks if we have a contact number and address for Phillip. Apparently Ewan McGregor wants to spend some time with him to master the character?

Steven (*genuinely surprised*): Really?

The Narrator hands Steven the letter.

Narrator: Here.

Steven skims the letter.

Steven: Well, I'll be damned. Do you think it's legitimate, or is it just part of the process to get Phillip to sign a release form for the film?

Narrator: Who knows? But just so you know, I'm drawing a line in the sand now. If Jim Carrey wants to come and spend a week living with us, he'll have to get his own cell. There isn't room for two of us on the floor.

The lights go out in Steven's cell. The Narrator steps out of Steven's cell to take center stage. A spotlight falls on him.

Narrator: Filming for *I Love You Phillip Morris* did indeed start in early 2008. At the very beginning of that year, however, we received a rare letter from Phillip detailing the week he and Ewan McGregor spent together at Phillip's home in Arkansas.

It's hard to know what inspired Phillip to write it. By then, I think it was clear to both of us that anything we once had was over. With the film in production though, both of us were reliving the past. Maybe that had something to do with it. The film title obviously didn't help matters.

On the other hand, by the time his letter arrived we hadn't physically seen each other for ten years. Maybe a little bit of him was showing off? Another part was probably just sharing his excitement with the only other person who knows exactly what he went through.

The Narrator takes a letter out of his jacket pocket and looks down at it. At the same time the Prisoner appears stage right and reads the letter he wrote.

Prisoner: "Dear Steven,"

"Ewan has just left for the airport! Ewan – did you hear me? We're on first-name terms now. Me and a Hollywood star on first-name terms! Can you believe it? Well, OK, maybe not a Hollywood star, but a British star anyway. He doesn't actually live in Hollywood. And he's Scottish rather than British. He did explain the difference to me, but I forget the details, something about Scotland being in northern England. Anyway, Ewan's just like Sean Connery only younger and thinner and with more hair."

"Excuse my writing, looking at that first paragraph I can see it's terrible, but the past few days have been amazing and I wanted to write and tell you all about it while everything's still fresh in my head."

"He arrived here on Monday in a rental-car that the studio paid for. Steven, over the past week the studio has paid for everything. We ate out three times a day. Breakfast, lunch and dinner! I think I've put on a few pounds, which as you know takes some doing. Normally I can't put on weight even if I try."

"Most of the week we just hung out. We saw some of the local sights together. We drove into Little Rock one day and walked along the river there. The rock itself was all boarded-up. They must be renovating it or something, but I mean how do you renovate a rock? All the time, Ewan was asking me questions about my childhood, the time I spent at school, how we met, what I thought of you and all the drama that followed on from that. He insisted I always tell him the truth, Steven, so that's mainly what I did. I told him how unfair I thought McNasty was in his book. I was happy Ewan wanted to see and hear the real, more human me."

"He repeated back a lot of what I said, which was kind of off-putting and a little annoying at times. He said he was trying to master my accent and claimed that learning words and phrases parrot-fashion worked well for him. Steven, you and I both know I do not have an accent. He has an accent. And if he spent the entire week trying to learn how to talk like me, I spent the week trying my hardest to understand a damned word he said. Why don't foreigners learn to speak English properly?"

"I'll confess that Ewan worried me a little. Sometimes he'd repeat what I said and he made me sound a lot more nelly than I really am. I think there must be something wrong with his hearing as well.

Anyway, after I realized what was happening, I butched it up for the rest of the time he was here. He also told me they're going to dye his hair blonde to match mine. I told him I'd dye my hair light brown and save him the trouble! We've laughed a lot over the past week."

"Steven, he asked me to describe my love for you. I found that difficult. Not the physical stuff, of course, that was easy. But it's hard to remember how I felt, especially given everything that's happened since. Prisons are odd places to fall in love, I suppose. Were our criminal records and location the only thing we had in common? Don't get me wrong, I remember being in love with you, it's just hard to explain to someone else how that feels now. Anyway, I think he got the picture. He seemed happy with all the answers I gave him."

"Oh my god, one night we rented *Star Wars* from the local Blockbuster store! You'll laugh, but I kept pausing it and asking him how they filmed the different scenes and what it was like. Apparently it was mostly done using blue screens, which I thought must have made it very hard. I mean, trying to act a part and there being nothing around you to help you. Did you know he rode a motorcycle from London to New York? Not over the Atlantic, of course. The other way: across Russia and Canada! I told him he should have taken a plane. It would have been a lot quicker."

"In other, exciting news, Ewan said the studio's happy to let me have a walk-on part in the film. They'll even pay me for it! That makes me a professional. You were always on at me to get a career. Maybe I'll try acting. Come to think of it, it'll be the first time I've worked since leaving jail. Maybe I should check it won't affect my disability before I say yes? Although I've already told Ewan I'll do it. I could always be in the film for free, right? Ewan also said he'd make sure I get an invite to the U.S. premiere, too. They want me to be available for interviews as well. Can you imagine? People interviewing me? I said that would be just fine."

"Before Ewan left, he gave me the address of his agent in London and another one he uses in Los Angeles. He said to stay in touch, which was nice. I don't know if we will. I mean, we had a great time and all, but I just don't think we will. We're very different people.

Anyway, the coming year is going to be a lot of fun for me and even after all the trouble you've put me through, over the years, I suppose I should say thank you. I also think it's karma. There has to be some good stuff as well to offset all the shit I've had to put up with, right?"

"Take care of yourself."

"Love, for old times' sake,"

"Phillip"

The Prisoner walks off stage right. The Narrator watches him go and then addresses the audience once more.

Narrator: A certain amount of closure came with that letter. Sexually, of course, I'd moved on. But with so much shared history and with the book out there and the film happening, some small part of what we once had lingered around.

Filming took place during 2008 and included shooting on location at a real prison unit. Not this one, obviously. Alvarado would never have allowed that. That would be like asking a man to kiss the boot you're about to wear before kicking him in the groin.

Then along came January, 2009. The greatest month in the history of America, for two main reasons.

Firstly, America finally saw the back of George W. Bush, the douchebag of a President it had somehow elected not once, but twice. That alone was cause for celebration. But at the same time our great nation proudly witnessed the inauguration of its first African-American president in Barack Obama. 'Hope and Change' were embraced and phrases like 'The War on Terror', 'Water Boarding' and 'W.O.M.D.' were thrown out with the garbage.

Of infinitely greater importance however, *I Love You Phillip Morris* received its world premiere at the 25th Sundance Film Festival.

ACT TWO

SCENE EIGHT

There is a small fanfare and a giant floor-to-ceiling banner of the I Love You Phillip Morris film poster rolls down from the ceiling to the stage floor.

A stagehand walks on and rolls out a red carpet in front of the banner. A second stagehand lays out two gold-colored metal posts and connects a red velvet rope between them. The Narrator and Steven walk around the front of the banner.

Steven: Wow. This is pretty swanky.

Narrator: How did you get out of your cell?

Steven: Well, we're not really here, are we?

Narrator: No, but even so.

Steven: Where are we again?

Narrator: The 25th Sundance Film Festival.

Steven: Right, and where does that take place?

Narrator: Utah.

Steven: The Mormon State? That seems a pretty odd place to have a film festival. It seems even odder that this would be the setting for the premiere of a gay love story.

Narrator: Remember, it's not a gay love story. It's just a love story.

Steven: Got it. So what happens here?

Narrator: Here, film executives and potential distributors get their first chance to look at the film.

Steven: Oh, so it's an industry thing?

Narrator: Pretty much.

Steven: How marvelous. Are the stars of the film here?

Narrator: They sure are.

Steven: Where are they?

Narrator: Well, over there... (*Some camera flashes go off*) That's Jim Carrey.

Steven: Oh, he looks taller than I thought he'd be.

Narrator: And there's Ewan McGregor.

Steven: And he looks shorter. Everyone looks so elegant though, don't they?

Narrator: Everyone, except you.

Steven (*looking at his prison clothes*): Oh my God, you're right. Wait here for a second, will you? While I change?

Steven disappears around the back of the film poster.

Narrator: While you change into what?

Steven reappears in a tuxedo after a moment.

Steven: Into this.

Narrator: Where did you get that?

Steven: Oh, this old thing? It's just something I've had in my closet for like, forever. I've just been waiting for the right occasion to wear it.

Narrator (*looking at his own suit*): Well, now I feel underdressed.

Steven: Well, why don't you go back there and slip into something more comfortable, too?

Narrator: Is there something back there for me?

Steven (*coyly*): There might be.

The Narrator disappears behind the banner. Steven remains on stage observing Jim Carrey and Ewan McGregor.

Steven (*to the Narrator*): Are they being interviewed?

Narrator (*from behind the screen*): Who?

Steven: Carrey and McGregor. It looks like they're talking to journalists.

Narrator (*still behind the screen banner*): Probably.

Steven: Why is no one interviewing us?

The Narrator reappears on stage in a tuxedo that matches Steven's.

Narrator: Because we're not famous.

Steven: We are famous! They're showing a film here about us! It's like showing a film about World War II with Winston Churchill present, and not using him for Q&A!

Narrator: Well, then it's because you're currently in a Texas jail.

Steven: Good point. Is Phillip here? The real one?

Narrator: I don't see him, but probably.

Steven: Well, that just seems unfair.

Narrator: I thought I was meant to be the fame-whore? When did you become one?

Steven: Ever since everyone else started getting a piece of the action and not us.

Narrator: Remember, fame's not the reason we did all of this.

Steven: I know, but it's all so pretty.

Narrator: Do you really want to be interviewed?

Steven: Duh. Yes.

Narrator: Well here, look, you be Jim Carrey and I'll interview you.

Steven (*excitedly*): Really?

Narrator: Yeah.

Steven: OK.

Narrator: I'll be the interviewer. Ready?

The Narrator holds an imaginary microphone in his hand.

Steven: Wait! Wait! Give me a second to get in character.

Narrator: Oh, for heaven's sake. Ready now?

Steven: Ready!

Narrator (*holding his imaginary microphone once more*): So, Mr Carrey, what did you find most challenging about playing Steven Russell?

Steven: Well Anderson, I'd have to say the most challenging aspect of playing Steven Russell was resisting the urge to touch myself whenever I was in character. I mean, that man just exudes confidence and sexuality.

Narrator: And what was it like to film inside a real prison?

Steven: Oh, Anderson it was hot. Like, hot, hot, hot! Like, really hot. The sin, the bars on the cell doors, and the enforced chastity. The sweat, the raging hormones, and all those buff guys! I mean, phew!

Narrator: I don't think Jim Carrey is gay.

Steven: I'm not, but when I take on a role like this I find it easier to stay in character even when we're not shooting, no pun intended. My approach necessitated a lot of man-on-man action in between takes. I wanted my portrayal to be totally authentic.

Narrator: I see, and what persuaded you to take on the role in the first place?

Steven: The money.

Narrator: I don't think Jim Carrey would say that.

Steven: No, but that's what I would say.

Narrator: But you're being him.

Steven: Oh. Well, I suppose something about the film being a new take on a familiar love story? Breaking down stereotypes, to humanize the plight of a nonviolent man in prison, the artistic challenge helping me to grow as an artist. That sort of thing.

Narrator: Awesome. I think you nailed it.

Steven: Hey! Why don't you be Ewan McGregor and I'll interview you?

Narrator: No. I can't do the accent.

Steven: Just try.

He lifts his own imaginary microphone to the Narrator's face.

Steven: So, Ewan, compare and contrast for us playing Phillip Morris with playing Obi-Wan Kenobi?

Narrator (*badly imitating Scottish accent*): Well, it's interesting that you mention that, Larry, because the characters share a number of wee facets in common: a childish innocence, belief in a higher power, and a fondness for waving phallic objects in public.

Steven: Ewan McGregor's German?

Narrator: I told you I can't do a Scottish accent!

Steven: Ewan, I understand you spent some time with the real Phillip Morris as preparation for playing the character.

Narrator (*back in a bad Scottish accent*): Aye. That I did.

Steven: What was the real Phillip Morris like?

Narrator: Well, I'll have to be honest with you and say he was a bit of a shit.

Steven: A bit of a shit, you say?

Narrator: Yes, just a wee bit. Not quite the Mayor of Shitsville, but definitely a lower-ranking publicly-elected town official.

Steven: I see. What would you say to people who argue that the gay undertones of this film make it unsuitable as a family film?

Narrator: I'd tell them to go fuck themselves. No, wait I wouldn't.

Steven: Good, because that's not going to help sell movie tickets.

Narrator: Exactly. I'd tell them to buy a ticket for the film...

Steven: Yes?

Narrator: And then to go fuck themselves.

Steven: And just one final question, Ewan?

Narrator: Yes, Larry?

Steven: Is it true that Scotsmen wear nothing beneath their kilts?

Narrator: Oh, no we have to have something to keep our haggis warm.

Steven: Oh, well, as a follow-up question then, if I might, Ewan: briefs or boxer shorts?

Narrator: Well, pantyhose, actually.

Steven: Oh my!

Narrator (*giggling*): And a garter! Come with me and I'll show you.

The Narrator runs off behind the banner like a schoolgirl with Steven chasing him. The movie poster rises and two stagehands come on and remove the red carpet, gold-colored posts and velvet ropes.

ACT TWO

SCENE NINE

The lights go on in Steven's cell. Steven is lying flat on his bed, dressed once again in his prison uniform. The Narrator takes center stage, addressing the audience. A spotlight shines on him.

Narrator: *I Love You Phillip Morris* was well-received and well-reviewed at the Sundance Film Festival. Yet, despite being eleven years in the making, the timing of its release was... terrible.

By early 2009, the fallout from the 2008 financial crisis had permeated through the financial system and was affecting real companies, including those in the entertainment business. Money was in short supply and everyone was risk-averse. Indeed, 2009 proved to be a low point for independent cinema. All the industry's mini-majors had closed and pretty much no one was buying independent films.

So, instead, *I Love You Phillip Morris* made its way around the film-festival circuit. After Sundance in January, it was shown at Berlin's European Film Market in February. In May it went to Cannes, in October to the Sao Paulo International Film Festival, and then in November to the Paris Gay and Lesbian Film Festival.

It wasn't until February 10, 2010, that *I Love You Phillip Morris* received its first national release...

Steven (*standing up*): Yesssssssssssssssss!

Narrator: ... in Belgium.

Steven (sitting down again): In Belgium?

Narrator: With concurrent releases in France and Switzerland.

Steven: What language do they even speak in Belgium?

Narrator: Finally, our story was being told to the general public.

Steven (*bitterly*): Yeah, in Belgium.

Narrator: Next came Russia, on February 11, and Taiwan on February 12. Those territories were followed by releases in Finland, Sweden, Estonia, Lithuania, Kazakhstan and Japan.

Steven: Are they going to show it anywhere that speaks English?

Narrator (*to Steven*): Will you wait a second? (*To the audience*) Then on March 17 *I Love You Phillip Morris* opened in Ireland and Great Britain.

Steven: Finally.

Major Linke (*from outside Steven's cell*): Come to the door.

Steven gets up and walks over to the door of his cell. He is handcuffed by Major Linke and led to the visitors' area. The Narrator addresses the audience.

Narrator: Prior to the film being released in Britain, we received an interview request from a British freelance journalist by the name of Diana Knight. Diana had requested an interview with us through the official channels, but had been frustrated by what she saw as a lack of co-operation from TDCJ officials. Being a resourceful woman, she decided to write to us directly. Soon after she was on a plane to Texas to meet with us.

Diana Knight enters from stage left and takes a seat on one side of the Plexiglas in the visitors' area. She is dressed smartly, perhaps a little overdressed for a prison visit. Steven arrives on his side and takes a seat. He picks up his receiver. Diana picks up hers.

Steven: Well, you must be Diana.

Diana (*in a muffled British accent*): And you must be Steven.

Steven: Well, now either you have a very strange accent or you've just come down with a cold?

Diana: Oh, I'm fine. It's just a spot of hay fever. They seem to be cutting the grass on the fields outside today and that, coupled with the heat, has set all my allergies off. Typically, I've left all my medication back in the hotel room.

Steven: Well, I'm sorry to hear that.

Diana: They wouldn't let me bring a Dictaphone in with me, so I'm going to have to take notes, I'm afraid. Do bear with me. First things first, tell me what you thought of the film?

Steven: The film?

Diana: Yes.

Steven: Well, to be honest with you…

Diana begins sneezing and reaches into her purse for some tissues, temporarily placing down the receiver.

Steven: … I haven't actually seen it.

Diana (*picking up her receiver again*): Sorry about that. I didn't catch your reply. Could you say it again?

Steven: What did you think of it?

186

Diana: Oh, I loved it. I thought it was clever, funny, and very modern, of course.

Steven: Well, it sounds like we have similar taste in movies, because that's exactly what I thought.

Diana: Oh, I'm so glad. How true is it to what happened to you in real life?

Steven: Let me level with you, Diana: it was like looking into a mirror. It felt like an out-of-body experience. It was surreal. Those all sound like clichés, but they're true. That they stuck so closely to the original story is also a testament to the high production values of everyone involved. Right down to the smallest detail.

Diana: What's your favorite moment in the film?

Steven: My favorite moment...

Diana: Yes, the bit that set goose bumps off all over your body.

Steven: For me it was the ending.

They are both silent for a moment.

Diana: You mean when everyone in the audience thinks you're dying of AIDS?

Steven (*pointing at her*): Bingo! Jim Carrey nailed it. So did the set designers and the location crew, because everything looked just the way I remember it.

Diana: Is it true you were never given an HIV test, even though you managed to convince everyone you had late-stage AIDS?

Steven: It's the gospel truth.

Diana (*wiping her nose*): How easy is it to fool people? I mean professionals, like that?

Steven: Easier than you'd think. Of course, my medical records showed that I'd had a couple of HIV tests and that I'd tested positive, but that's because I arranged to have them say that.

There were a couple of scary moments when they wanted to test me again, but whenever they did I just said I wasn't up to it. I was emaciated by then. I'd starved myself to look the part. It was easy to believe I was ill, so why wouldn't they believe me?

Diana: Have you had any reaction from people here in prison who have seen the film? Other inmates or perhaps from members of the prison's staff?

Steven: Not really. I don't have much contact with other people here in prison. I'm waiting for the day that the Warden here gets to see it. I think he's going to really enjoy it.

Diana: Do you blame the state of Texas for your current predicament?

Steven (*sighing*): The only person I can blame is myself. I understand why the people around me have reacted the way they have. Personally, I don't think I should still be behind bars, given the nonviolent nature of my crimes, but I get why some people here in Texas might think I should be. I embarrassed a lot of people, doing what I did. And they think I need to be punished.

Diana: Is it right that you're currently housed on death row?

Steven: It is. They think it's the safest place for me to be. Let me correct that. They think it's the securest place for me to be. It's certainly not a safe place for anyone.

Diana: So you're surrounded by people who have been convicted of murder?

Steven: Yes, ma'am.

Diana: Do you believe in the death penalty, Mr Russell? The last time Britain executed a felon was in 1964. We made capital punishment illegal five years later.

Steven: I believe in the sanctity of life, that no one has the right to take another person's life. Let a person convicted of a capital crime spend their life in a concrete box, like I am. As long as the prison staff do their job, they'll never be able to escape from here. I'm a firm believer that two wrongs make a right.

Diana (*wiping her nose*): And what about your wrongs? After this film I would have thought people would be calling for your release. Is that something you ever envisage happening? Finally getting out of your concrete box the legitimate way?

Steven: It would be nice, I don't deny that. I see no sense in keeping me in here, but as to when it might happen, I have no idea and it's not something I'm pinning my hopes on. For now I'm making the best of a bad situation. I listen to the radio, I keep myself up to date on current affairs, and I do a lot of reading. Compared to some people in this country, I don't have it too bad. Although let me state for the record, I believe enforced isolation is a very cruel and unusual punishment.

Diana: Do you have any thoughts about what you'd do if you ever got out? Would you travel? I can imagine you'd like to get about a bit, having been in one place for so long.

Steven: If I'm ever released on parole, I'd have to stay here in Texas. That's OK with me, I like Texas and most Texans. I suppose I could become the resident expert on jailbreaks for some cable news network, but more realistically I'd happily settle for a quiet life somewhere where I can have my own garden and grow fresh fruit and vegetables. I mean, if and when I get out of here, I'm going to be an old man.

Diana: Do you ever wish you'd settled for the whole nine-to-five thing?

Steven: That's an interesting question because it assumes I chose the life I did because so-called ordinary life bored me. I certainly don't think I'm too good for a nine-to-five job, or anything like that. I just think I was underappreciated. Whenever I broke the law, it was the result of a simple weighing up of all the options available to me. None of the legitimate options recognized the considerable skills that I have or the risks I was prepared to take.

Diana: So working nine-to-five would have left you... underemployed?

Steven: Let's just say I sometimes felt underutilized. A little bored, maybe. Not that I miss the drama and stress of my previous life. I quite like the quiet life now, the lack of decisions, and not having to look over my shoulder. I certainly don't miss the pounding headaches and adrenaline rushes. But that's because I'm older and I've seen the other side. It's not greener. I didn't know that way back when.

It's actually a miracle I'm still healthy. When you think of everything I've done to my body. I once injected myself with enough insulin to put me in a coma, just so I'd be taken to hospital rather than jail. Starving yourself typically isn't the route to a long life either. Nor attempting suicide. How about you? Do you ever wish you'd become a conman rather than a journalist?

Diana: Sometimes. Usually when one of my kids has just vomited and I'm mopping up the sick. But I get to meet some pretty interesting people in my job. I suppose you do too.

Steven: You'd think so, right? But living permanently on death row is a bit like working in a pet shop selling puppies. You learn not to get too attached to them because, sooner or later, someone's going to walk in here, carry them out and you're never going to see them again.

The lights go out in the visitors' area. Major Linke takes Steven back to his cell.

ACT TWO

SCENE TEN

The light comes on in Steven's cell.

Narrator (*to the audience*): The article that interview became didn't turn out too badly. And with the film finally released in an English-speaking market, two if you count Ireland, critics were also able to chime in on the film, which meant...

Major Linke (*from outside the cell door*): Mail call!

Narrator (*to the audience*): ... Reviews.

Steven goes over to his letterbox and picks up a letter.

Steven (*to the Narrator*): It's from Glenn Ficarra.

Narrator: And what does Glenny-boy have to say for himself?

Steven (*reading out loud*): "Dear Steven,"

"I thought you'd like to know that *I Love You Phillip Morris* has now been released across most of Europe. I attach some magazine and newspaper reviews of the movie, which I think you will enjoy. Those enclosed are from Britain. Glenn and I particularly like the *Daily*

Post's review."

"Best wishes,"

"Glenn."

Narrator: Oh, this is just like Christmas.

Steven hands him two of the four reviews enclosed.

Narrator: Go on, you read one first.

Steven: OK. This one is from *Film Magazine*, which Glenn says is Britain's pre-eminent movie magazine. They gave the film four stars out of five!

Narrator: Four stars? That's one each for Jim Carrey, Ewan McGregor, you and I!

Steven (*clearing his throat*): "One of the best comedies you'll see this year. A glorious mix of classic Carrey outrageousness with a heart-warming and very modern love story." Modern - that's the same word Diana Knight used. When did 'gay' and 'modern' become synonymous?

Narrator: Beats me. I always thought the Greeks invented homosexuality?

Steven: You read one of yours.

Narrator: OK. This one is from *The Sentinel*. They also give the film four stars out of five. Glenn, or I suppose it could have been John, has scribbled 'liberal newspaper' across the top, in pencil.

Steven: What did they say?

Narrator: "Jim Carrey's irrepressible, elastic facial expressions reach new levels of hysteria and frenzied inadequacy in this outlandish comedy that's based on a true story. Steven Russell..." Oh, my god, that's us!

Steven: I know!

Narrator: "… brilliantly portrayed by Carrey, is a conman, an entrancingly believable fantasist, former family man and police officer who comes out as gay, before finally being arrested and imprisoned in Texas for insurance fraud. There he finds his true love…" Aw, they're talking about me.

Steven: I think you'll find they mean Phillip.

Narrator: "This is the youthful, coy, angelic Phillip Morris, aptly played by Ewan McGregor…" Oh. You were right.

"Their dynamic is chaotic and tumultuous, a love that neither of them seem to fully comprehend. It is this confused and disorderly quality that tells you this is a tale drawn straight out of real life. 'Sometimes you've got to shave a little off the puzzle-piece to make it fit,' suggests Steven at one point. Everything comes together nicely in this film."

My other one's from *London's Evening News*:

"Jim Carrey brings his trademark charm and zaniness to the improbable-but-true world of Steven Russell… He also brings a Hollywood name to a film about two gay men in love. It feels like a love story for the new century, to be enjoyed by anyone who has ever had the pleasure of falling head-over-heels in love."

Now I feel all gooey inside. London has always been one of my favorite cities.

Steven: We've never been there! Here's the last one. It's from the *Daily Post*. Glenn has written in red ink across the top and underlined it three times: 'Britain's literary equivalent of *Fox News*'.

Narrator (*laughing*): I'm guessing that they didn't like it then.

Steven: Rating: 'Turkey'. No stars out of five.

Narrator: Really? Did they see the same film those other three critics saw?

Steven: "Just as awful as *Happy Endings*," I'm guessing that was another film they must have reviewed, "and no less perplexing, is *I Love You Phillip Morris.*"

"The now well-past-his-best Jim Carrey grimaces and pouts his way through this appalling comedy, the sheer dreadfulness of which cannot be excused by it allegedly being based on real life."

Narrator: Grimaces and pouts?

Steven: Like this...

Steven demonstrates both grimacing and pouting.

Narrator: I know what the words mean, you dummy.

Steven: "Carrey plays a self-obsessed and mentally unstable con-artist who abandons his wife and daughter in order to live a debt-financed, flamboyantly gay lifestyle with, respectively, an AIDS victim and another career criminal."

Narrator: Flamboyantly gay lifestyle?

Steven: It gets better, "Ewan McGregor plays Carrey's 'love interest'" They put that in inverted commas. "In another of his phony and wooden performances, which includes a simply laughable attempt at an American accent."

Narrator: Ouch.

Steven: "Some will wince at the graphic, on-screen, in-your-face depiction of gay sex, but you don't need to be homophobic to dislike Steven Russell, the character Carrey plays."

Narrator: Although I'm sure it helps.

Steven: "Unbelievably, the writing-directing team of Ficarra and Requa seem to think Russell's a misunderstood rogue, instead of a sociopathic conman with all the appeal of a cockroach."

"This is the kind of pathetically sad, wannabe indie-film that former A-listers only make when their careers are in freefall. It's a frightfully misguided mix of would-be comedy, drama, supposed romance, and toe-curling sex."

Are you ready for the finale?

Narrator: Give it to me.

Steven: "Face-achingly unfunny and morally bankrupt, the film fails in every department. Burn the money you would have spent seeing this movie. It will be more rewarding."

The Narrator rushes over to see the review for himself.

Narrator: Oh my god, that one is such a keeper!

Steven: What kind of people read the *Daily Post*?

Narrator: Never mind that, what kind of people write for the *Daily Post*? I thought all the Nazis fled to Argentina after the war?

Steven: At least the journalist is being paid. Who pays money to read that kind of bigotry?

Narrator: People who think your biggest crime was choosing a flamboyantly gay lifestyle over your wife and daughter?

Steven: Ex-wife. Do you think the reviewer stayed for the whole film?

Narrator: Possibly. Unless Jesus appeared and told him to leave halfway through. Either way I'm sure he was sick all over his popcorn.

Steven: So, overall, what do you think?

Narrator: It's a hit!

Steven: Well, that's what I get from these three. Not so much from that one.

Narrator: Remember, every film has a target audience. Who did you think was going to go see it anyway? Certainly not the bigots and Bible-bashers. It'll be the lefties, the laid-backs, the liberals, the students, the gays, the Democrats and the arts-theater crowds. They'll love it. In Britain that's basically everyone apart from *Daily Post* readers.

Steven: I suppose, but I don't think Alvarado is any of those. And he's certainly not British.

The Narrator addresses the audience.

Narrator: Unfortunately, Steven had a point. Thus far, the movie still hadn't been released in America. That meant that not only had Alvarado not had a chance to see it, but neither had his friends, his family, his colleagues, his ex-colleagues, his neighbors or his golfing buddies. And that, after all, is why we wrote the book in the first place and why we got so excited when they made it into a film. The months that followed brought false dawn after false dawn.

On March 24, *I Love You Phillip Morris* was released in The Philippines. A day later it was released in the Czech Republic, and by the end of the month it was showing in Iceland.

By the end of April it had also opened in Italy, Denmark, the Netherlands, Portugal and Germany.

Steven: But when are they going to show it here?

Narrator (*still to the audience*): In May it opened in Hong Kong and

Poland, followed by releases in Brazil and Croatia in June.

Steven: Did we miss something? When John and Glenn came to see us, they did fly in from Hollywood, didn't they? The one in California?

Narrator: July saw the film hit Israel, South Korea, Greece, Hungary, Austria and Mexico.

Steven: Isn't there another California in Mexico? Do they live and work there maybe?

Narrator: Then, very astutely, Spain began showing the film on Friday, August 13.

Steven: OK. That was clever.

Narrator: Argentina and Singapore got the film in September, but still there was no sign of the film being released anywhere in the U.S.

Steven: OK. That's it. I've had enough.

Narrator (*to Steven*): What do you mean you've had enough?

Steven: Get John and Glenn on the phone, right now.

Narrator: Well, I would, but we don't have a phone and you're not allowed to use the phones available for inmates.

Steven: I don't care. Get them on the phone.

Narrator: OK, but where am I supposed to get a phone from?

Steven points downstage to the Warden's office.

Steven: There are three of them over there on the table.

The Narrator looks around Steven's cell.

Narrator: What table?

Steven (*pointing across the stage*): That table, you idiot!

Narrator (*confused*): That's Walden Alvarado's office.

Steven: Yes, but in this scene it's going to have to double as John and Glenn's office as well. Now, go over there, fetch the phone and call John and Glenn.

The Narrator reluctantly walks across the stage, picks up one of the phones from Warden Alvarado's office and brings it back to Steven's cell.

Narrator: Do you have their number or do you just want me to guess?

Steven: Of course I don't have their number. Get it from directory assistance or something.

Narrator: Fine. Hello, operator? (*Improbably*) Could you connect me to John Requa's office in Hollywood? (*To Steven*) I really don't think this is going to work.

Steven: Of course it'll work. That's the magic of theater.

Narrator (*to the operator, surprised*): You can? Oh, that's great. Yes, please, if you would. Thank you. (*To Steven*) It's ringing.

Steven: Finally.

One of the remaining two phones in Walden Alvarado's office starts ringing and John Requa appears from stage right to answer it. He picks up the receiver.

John: This is John Requa.

Narrator: John, I'm calling from Steven Russell's office. Will you hold to speak with him, please?

John: Sure. I'll get Glenn on the line too. (*He shouts offstage*) Glenn!

Glenn Ficarra enters from stage right. He picks up the other desk phone so that both of them are now holding a receiver.

Narrator: Transferring you now.

The Narrator hands the phone to Steven.

Steven: Hi guys!

John: Hi Steven. It's John. I have Glenn on the line too.

Glenn: Hi Steven.

Steven: Awesome. Great to speak to you both again! It's been a while. I'll get straight to the point. I've been following all the national releases for your film, I imagine the United Nations is buzzing with people talking about our movie. Anyway, I was just wondering if there was any reason why it hasn't been released here in America yet?

John (*sighing*): Oh, Steven, I don't know what to tell you…

Glenn: Yeah, it's kind of a long and slightly embarrassing story.

Steven sits down on his bed and crosses his legs.

Steven: Well, I've got plenty of time and it can't be more embarrassing than having your nut-sack searched for contraband.

John: True. Well, the thing is… There's no easy way to put this, so I'll just say it. We kind of sold the U.S. distribution rights to a company that didn't exist.

Steven: You did what?

Glenn: You have to remember, all the big distribution companies that were interested at Sundance wanted to test-market the film. They were nervous about the gay subject matter. They wanted us to jump through all of these hoops before they would commit to us.

John: Well, we eventually found a guy who wasn't bothered about any of that and who loved the film. And he appeared to run a legitimate distribution company. The only downside was, as we later found out, he turned out to be a conman.

Steven: You sold the U.S. distribution rights for our film to a conman?

John (*laughing*): Right? What are the odds? We make a film about a serial fraudster, felon and prison escapee, and we end up inadvertently selling the American rights to a conman using an assumed name? Talk about life-imitating-art-imitating-life. I mean, go figure.

Steven: Would you both excuse me for one second?

John and Glenn (*politely*): Sure.

Steven hands the receiver to the Narrator, walks over to his cell wall and bangs his head against the wall.

Narrator: Don't be so hard on yourself. It's only eleven years' work down the drain.

John (*hearing the thudding*): Steven? Steven, are you OK?

Glenn: We can hear banging… Steven?

John: Hello?

Steven walks back over to the Narrator and takes back the receiver.

Narrator (*to Steven*): Better?

Steven (*to the Narrator*): Much.

Glenn: Are you still there?

Steven (*back on the phone*): Sorry about that, there was just something I needed to take care of. So what happens now?

John: Well, the good news is that once the financiers were on to him, he skipped the country.

Glenn: Yeah, he's probably in Mexico right about now.

Steven: You're not though, right? You're in the California that's in America?

Glenn: Um, yeah.

John: So his con actually failed. Only unfortunately, by then, a lot of the paperwork and contracts had been signed, which meant that it all had to be undone before we could sell the rights to someone else.

Steven: Right. Someone who isn't a conman, maybe?

John: I mean, preferably. Yes.

Steven: Just so I understand, why would a conman try and get the rights to distribute a film? What exactly was the con he was trying to pull?

John: He was trying to pull a fast one. See, when you agree to distribute a film, you also get the rights to distribute the video, although nowadays it's mainly DVDs and Blu-rays rather than videotapes.

Well, companies typically on-sell the rights to a video distribution company, thus recouping some or all of what they paid for the film in the first place. The guy we were dealing with didn't actually have any money to pay for the film rights. His plan was to try and on-sell the video rights before he had to part with any cash for the film itself.

Glenn: There's a chance he might have been thinking he could just use that money to pay us for the U.S. distribution rights. So it could have just been a cash-flow thing...

John (*to Glenn*): But that would be really dodgy anyway…

Steven: Or more likely he was planning to just flee the country with the money he got from the video rights without paying you guys a dime?

John: Yeah, that's more likely. Anyway, he was apparently saying things like, "The check's in the mail," and all that. It was very shady. And by the time the lawyers got the movie back from him, we'd basically lost a year.

Glenn: There is some good news, though.

Steven: There is?

John: There is. The film's getting a U.S. release in three months' time.

Steven: It is? In December?

Glenn: In December.

Steven: In Houston?

John (*laughing*): It'll definitely be shown in Houston.

Steven: Would you guys give me another second?

John and Glenn: Sure.

Steven (*aside in a silent shout*): Yesssssssssss! (*Calmly, to John and Glenn*) That's great news!

John (*apologizing*): Look, Steven, we're sorry it's taken so long. I'm sure you're keen for all your friends and family to see it…

Steven: Something like that.

Glenn: And we're sorry we weren't more forthcoming with what was happening, but we hope you can understand. The lawyers wanted us to keep it under wraps while there was still a chance of catching the guy.

Steven: Do you have his real name? Maybe I know him?

John (*laughing*): You probably do.

Glenn: Steven, we need to head off for a meeting, so take care of yourself, you hear? And maybe we'll see you at one of the U.S. showings in December?

Steven: Sounds good to me.

John: Goodbye, Steven.

Glenn: It's been great chatting with you.

John: And if we don't see you, have a Merry Christmas!

Steven: Thanks guys. Thanks for everything.

They all hang up. John and Glenn leave stage right. The Narrator returns the phone Steven was using to Warden Alvarado's office.

Narrator: It's happening, right?

Steven: It's actually happening.

Narrator: In December?

Steven: In December.

Narrator: First item on the agenda, then?

Steven: Find out when and where the film is showing in Houston and send Warden Alvarado a pair of tickets for him and his wife.

Narrator: Yes.

Steven: We can ask Sally to look it up and buy the tickets for us!

Narrator: Do you think we should?

Steven: There's nothing illegal about sending someone free movie tickets.

Narrator: I guess not.

Steven: Oh, man. If this doesn't send him over the edge, I don't know what will.

The Narrator steps out to center stage and addresses the audience.

Narrator: And so it was on December 3, 2010, *I Love You Phillip Morris* was released across America. The arts-cinema crowd, the gays and the liberals all went and saw it. Our friends, family, Gabriel Unit employees, and quite a few people I'd done jail-time with, also made the trek to their local movie theater to see it. How do I know? Because most of them wrote to tell us about it.

The sliding door to Steven's cell opens.

Major Linke: Surprise!

Major Linke enters carrying a huge sack of mail.

Steven: Aren't you supposed to shout 'mail call' or something?

Major Linke: Oh, you have most definitely got mail. And I'm not going to spend half an hour poking all this through the letterbox.

Narrator (*to Steven*): Oh, it's just like the scene in *Harry Potter* when the letters fly out of the chimney!

Steven: We haven't seen any of the *Harry Potter* films.

Narrator: Then it's just like it is in the book!

Steven: I'll take your word for it.

Major Linke empties the bag on the cell floor.

Major Linke: I'm going to have to keep the sack.

Steven: No problem.

Major Linke: Give me a shout in an hour or so and I'll come back and pick up all the envelopes.

Steven: Sure thing.

Major Linke (*coyly*): Steven? Can I ask you a favor?

Steven: A favor? Sure.

Major Linke: I kind of told my nephew I'd get him your autograph. If I bring in a flyer for the movie or something, would you sign it for him? He hasn't seen the movie of course. He's too young to see anything like that. But he knows they made a film about you. And I told him that I sort of knew you.

Steven: I'd be happy to.

Major Linke: Thanks.

Major Linke leaves the cell. The cell door slides shut behind him.

Narrator: Well, where do we start?

Steven (*looking down at the huge pile*): At the top, I guess.

They start opening the letters.

Narrator: "Dear Steven, I'm writing to tell you that God hates you... Blah, blah, blah... Brimstone, fire, eternal damnation... Blah, blah,

blah…Yours sincerely, ugly and bigoted from Alabama." Well, that was a good one to start with.

The Narrator discards the letter.

Steven: "Dear Mr Russell, I have just seen *I Love You Phillip Morris* and I wanted to tell you that I thought you were excellent. The plot was very believable and I can see how you managed to trick so many people. You must be very clever, though I imagine it helps that you look so much like Jim Carrey."

Steven discards the letter.

Narrator: "Dear Mr Russell, Hogwarts School of Witchcraft and Wizardry looks forward to welcoming you this coming semester…"

Steven (*excitedly*): Really?

Narrator: No. It's another one from the God squad. Is there like a hate club they all belong to or something?

Steven: It's called church.

Narrator: Why do they waste their time?

The Narrator discards the letter.

Steven: "Dear Steven, *I Love You Phillip Morris* was so hot. I particularly liked the scene where Ewan McGregor went down on you in the boat. If I'd been in that boat with you I would have…" (*He keeps reading but only mumbles the words*)… Wow. I'm keeping this one for later.

Steven stuffs the letter under the pillow on his bed.

Narrator: This one's from Russia. "Dearest Russell. I am likings your film *I Like You Mr Morris* and am offering my services if you ever come to Russia. I am having good connections with Russian mafia which I am thinkings could be beneficial for both of us." Well, that might come in handy one day, I suppose?

The Narrator throws away the letter.

Steven: This one's from Nebraska. "Dear Steven, I hope you don't mind me writing to you, but I recently saw the film about your life at a small movie theatre in Omaha. I wanted to tell you that it gave me hope. I'm eighteen years old and I still live with my parents. Although I know I'm gay, I haven't done anything about it yet, but your film showed me that I need to be true to who I am and start living my life. Obviously the stuff about all your crimes and you getting locked up was a bit off-putting, but what really touched me was that your motivation for breaking the law… was love."

The Narrator walks over to Steven.

Narrator: Aw.

Steven: It kind of makes everything seem worthwhile, doesn't it?

Narrator (*snatching the letter*): Who are you kidding? We didn't do this for the good of humanity. We're in this for the fame and the money.

Steven: Fair point. What's this one? "Dear Steven… will you marry me?"

Steven throws the letter away and picks up another.

"Dear Steven. Could you send me $25,000 for my son's operation?"

Steven throws the letter away as well.

Narrator: "Dear Mr Russell, I know you think you're gay, but I think you just haven't met the right woman yet. I think I might be the right woman for you."

Steven: Is she rich?

Narrator: She doesn't say.

Steven: Is her father the Governor of Texas?

Narrator: I'm guessing not.

Steven: Does she have a dick?

The Narrator examines a photo included in the letter.

Narrator: If she does, it's very small.

Steven: Well then, I can't see it working. Hey, this one's from John Requa!

The Narrator throws his letter away.

Narrator: What does he have to say for himself?

Steven: It's a collection of U.S. reviews for the film.

Narrator: Is there a letter with it?

Steven: No, he's just scribbled on the top of the first one. "Thought you'd like these. Glenn and I have been very busy with the U.S. release. Will write more at a later date. Best wishes, John."

Narrator: Good, I love reviews. Well, I like the positive ones at least. Give me a couple, let's read them out loud again.

Steven hands him some and keeps some for himself.

Narrator: OK, this one is… It's *The New York Tribune*!

The Narrator fans himself with the clipping.

"Carrey's take on Steven Russell, an infamous career-criminal and confidence-trickster currently serving a 144-year sentence in a Texas jail, supercharges *I Love You Phillip Morris*, a nail-biting comedy that markets itself as an 'improbable but true story.'"

"Jim Carrey's transmogrification…"

Steven: What?

Narrator: It means change.

Steven: Why not just say change?

Narrator: It's *The New York Tribune*!

(*Continuing*) "… into a toned-down version of his usual screen persona, marks *I Love You Phillip Morris* as the best Jim Carrey movie in a while. With his frantic stare, Cheshire-Cat smile, hyper-energetic body language and gift for instant self-transformation, Mr Carrey has seldom been more mesmerizing."

Yay!

The Narrator gives himself a small round of applause.

Steven: This one is from *The Manhattanite*:

"In spite of its title, *I Love You Phillip Morris* is not a politically-incorrect declaration of love to the tobacco industry. It is something altogether more implausible: a chance to see Ewan McGregor make out with Jim Carrey."

Narrator: I feel dirty just thinking about it.

Steven: "One might call the film a genuine love story, its passion undeterred by the confines of prison, the strain of distance or the finality of death. Or one might agree with a line delivered by Phillip in the movie: 'Enough romance. Let's fuck!'"

Narrator: Would it be wrong to get turned on watching an actor, playing you, having sex with another actor, playing your ex-boyfriend? I think I may need professional help with that one.

Steven: "*I Love You Phillip Morris* might also be trumpeted as progress in Hollywood's heel-dragging crawl towards sexual fairness; the movie upholds the right of gay men to be liars, thieves and scoundrels just like the rest of us. It makes you proud to be an American."

Narrator: Stop it. I'm blushing.

Steven: Me too.

Narrator: This one's from the *Chicago Telegraph*. It's a bad photocopy though and I can't read the text, but they gave it three-and-a-half stars out of five.

Steven: *The Philadelphia Inquisitor*: "Carrey flaunts his usual array of tricks, but his performance in this film has real soul - definitely the best thing he's done since *Eternal Sunshine of the Spotless Mind*."

Narrator: *NPR* gave the film a score of 8 out of 10 and said: "Carrey and McGregor are a riot of fun in this straight take on a gay love story with a comically criminal plot line."

Steven picks up a new letter and pauses.

Steven: This one's from *The Houston Journal*.

Narrator: Really? What did they say?

Steven: They gave it two-and-a-half stars out of five.

Narrator: Only two-and-a-half?

Steven: "Based on a book by former *Houston Journal* reporter Steve McVicker, *I Love You Phillip Morris* is a bit of a strange fruit: a crazy tragedy-cum-romance inspired by real-life Texan bad-boy Steven Russell, his one-time cellmate, Phillip Morris, and their many capers carried out in the name of love."

"To enjoy this film we need to accept Russell as both a fake and a romanticist. We also need to welcome a plot that manipulates and obfuscates us as much as any of Steven's victims."

"Jim Carrey is masterful as Russell, radiating sensitivity and bluster, often within moments of each other, but he's let down by sloppy and uneven direction."

Narrator: Ouch.

Steven: "Since we can't get to grips with the story-telling, we can't get to grips with Steven, making it hard to care very much what happens to him."

Narrator: Hard to care?

Steven: That's what it says.

Narrator: Was McVicker well-liked at *The Houston Journal?*

Steven: He never struck me as the kind of man who would have upset anyone.

Narrator: So what is it? Jealousy? He left the *Journal* and had his book turned into a film? Is it sour grapes?

Steven: Who knows? Look, it's not important.

Narrator: Of course, it's important! That's the review everyone we know is going to read.

Steven: Only the people we know in Texas.

Narrator: Which is everyone that counts.

Steven: It's a tiny setback. Everyone that knows us has either seen the film already or is going to see it no matter what *The Houston Journal* says.

Narrator: It's just, I don't know... annoying.

Steven: There's nothing we can do about it now. You know how these things are. They're hit and miss. We could have gotten a completely different review if the paper had sent someone else. As it is they sent this guy. (*He checks and corrects himself*) Girl, actually.

Narrator (*slumping down on the bunk*): Whatever.

Steven: Most of the reviews have been glowing.

Narrator: I just would have preferred that one to be better.

Steven: Don't let it get to you. Are you going to help me get through the rest of these?

Narrator: Yeah, in a bit. Let me stew for a moment. (*He gestures to the envelope that contained the reviews John Requa sent*). Are there any more in there?

Steven: Reviews? No, I think that was all of them. Oh, there's one still in there.

Narrator (*feigning surprise*): Is there?

Steven: Oh, it's not a review.

Narrator: What is it then?

Steven: It must be a companion piece to that *Houston Journal* review. It's a phone interview. (*Pause*) With Phillip.

Narrator: And what does the lovely Phillip have to say for himself?

Steven: Give me a chance to read it and I'll tell you.

Steven reads the letter silently to himself.

Steven: Hmm.

Narrator: What?

Steven: "Phillip: I would often sit in my cell at night, crying. It was nothing to do with Steve and everything to do with being wrongfully convicted and sucked into all of his mess." (*To the Narrator*) Wrongly accused, my ass! He went along with everything we did!

Narrator (*pointing*): There's more. Read the last bit.

Steven: "Journal: How do you feel about this story being out there in public?"

"Phillip: I'm over the moon about it. Finally, people are going to see me exactly as I am: just another one... (*Pause*) Just another one of Steve's victims. (*Pause*) I've seen the film with close friends and members of my family, none of whom really knew what that man put me through. Well, now they know."

The Narrator stands as Steven sits down quietly on the bunk.

Narrator: Are you OK?

Steven: I'm fine.

Narrator: Are you sure?

Steven: More than sure. (*Pause*) You knew that was in there, didn't you?

Narrator: Yes.

Steven: Have you always known he would say that?

The Narrator nods.

Steven: Is that it, then? It feels like it is.

Narrator: It's just the end of a chapter. And the beginning of a new one.

Steven: Life after Phillip Morris?

Narrator: It's as good a working title as any.

Steven: Maybe it's about time.

Narrator: It's more than about time.

Steven: So, who replaces him? The Latino?

Narrator: Do you need to replace him? It seems to me that relationships for you, I should say for us, are like drugs. We crave them, but they're no good for us.

Steven: We're going cold turkey?

Narrator: I want us to define who we are, not by whom we love or protect, but by what we say and do. Anyway, you act like we have a choice other than cold turkey in here.

Steven: And we still have family, right?

Narrator: The ones God gave us and the new ones that will come into our life. Some because of the film.

They sit in silence for a moment.

Steven: Do you think Alvarado even saw the film?

There is movement at the door to Steven's cell and the lights flicker on and off.

Narrator: I think we might be about to find out.

ACT TWO

SCENE ELEVEN

Major Linke: Roll 24!

Lt. Herrera (*in the distance*): Rolling 24.

The door to Steven's cell slides open and in steps Warden Alvarado and another man, the Double. Major Linke stays outside the cell by the door.

Steven: Warden Alvarado, what an unexpected honor. Have you come to ask for my autograph as well?

Double (*to the Warden, hissing*): That's not him! It's an imposter. It's not Russell, I tell you! He's escaped, he must have!

Narrator (*whispering to Steven*): Who's the crazy guy with him?

Steven (*to the Narrator*): What guy?

Double (*to the Warden*): Who's he talking to? Is he talking to you? You're the Warden. He needs to show you some respect!

Narrator: Are you seeing this?

Steven (*to the Narrator*): I have no idea what you're talking about.

Warden (*to Steven*): No, Russell, I have not come to get ask for your autograph. I have come to bid you farewell.

Steven: Am I going somewhere? Is it Jamaica?

Warden: Oh, you're not going anywhere. But I am.

The Warden and the Double glance down at the pile of letters on the cell floor.

Double (*to the Warden*): Look at all the mail! Was it all read? Was it checked for contraband? Your staff are useless. Did they check properly? What if they didn't? What then?

Narrator (*whispering to Steven*): You really can't see that guy?

Steven (*to the Narrator*): I have no idea who or what you're talking about.

Warden (*to Steven*): Well then, let me spell it out for you…

Steven: Sorry, I didn't mean you. I was talking to…

Double (*to the Warden*): Talking to who? Who was he talking to? Does he have someone hidden in here? Under the bed maybe? Maybe it's his accomplice!! Get them to check!! Get them to check now!

Steven: … Myself. I was talking to myself.

Warden: Is everything OK, Russell?

Steven: Everything's fine, warden. Is everything OK with you?

Warden: Yes.

Double (*to the Warden*): Something's not quite right about all this. Maybe we shouldn't tell him. Maybe we should just leave quietly?

Warden: I'm leaving Gabriel Unit.

Steven: You're leaving? Have you been reassigned?

Warden: No.

Double (*to the Warden*): You don't have to tell him. Not if you don't want to.

Warden: I'm... retiring.

Steven: You're retiring?

Warden: Yes.

Narrator (*to Steven*): Look, I know this might sound strange, but there is a guy standing to the Warden's left who looks just like him.

Steven (*whispering to the Narrator*): Why would that seem strange, after I've put up with you for the past twelve years?

Narrator (*to Steven*): Are you absolutely sure you can't see him?

Steven: Positively.

Narrator (*to Steven*): Well, I can see him clear as day.

Double (*to the Warden*): He's acting very suspiciously. You should call the guard. Get some handcuffs on him in case he tries something.

Warden (*ignoring the Double*): I'm finally going to enjoy the fruits of my labor. While you remain here, enjoying the fruits of yours.

Narrator (*to Steven*): I'm willing to bet good money he's seen the film.

Steven (*to the Warden*): I'm sure your wife is looking forward to seeing you more.

Double (*to the Warden*): Tell him. Tell him now. We won't be forgetting about all of his little tricks, will we?

Warden (*to Steven*): I'll still be checking in on you from time to time, Russell. Every Friday the 13th. Whoever your new Warden is, he'll be getting a call from me.

Steven: Well, I'm sure the new guy will appreciate that.

Narrator (*to Steven*): Ask him if he saw the film.

Steven: Did you get the tickets I sent you, by the way? The movie tickets?

Double (*pointing at Steven*): He sent them! I knew it was him!

Warden: Yes and no. It would be improper for a Warden to accept a gift from one of his inmates. And I guessed you had a hand in it.

Double: A gift? Puh! The film was full of lies, filth and half-truths!

Steven: Oh, that's a shame. You did see the film though, right?

Double (*to the Warden*): Deny it. Don't give him the satisfaction!

Warden: I did see it.

Double (*whining*): You don't have to tell him!

Warden: I didn't like it.

Steven: You didn't? Was the subject matter a little too close to home for you?

Warden: I thought the whole thing was a colossal waste of time and money. I'm sure the company that made it feels the same way.

Steven: They're quite pleased, actually.

Warden: Your character certainly comes across as unlikeable, though of course that came as no surprise.

Steven (*pointing to the letters at his feet*): I'm not sure the people who wrote these agree with you.

Warden: Most of them are idiots. Certainly not people that matter.

Narrator (*to Steven*): He's read them all. Personally.

Steven (*to the Narrator, out of the corner of his mouth*): You think?

Narrator (*to Steven*): Without a shadow of a doubt.

Warden: I've said it before, Russell, but you don't seem to hear me. You're not special. You're not a celebrity.

Steven: *The Discovery Channel* seems to think otherwise. They want to do a half-hour episode on me as part of their *True Crime* series.

Double: He's lying. We'd have seen a letter or something.

Warden: No one watches *The Discovery Channel*, Russell.

Narrator (*to Steven*): Ask him who his friend is.

Steven (*to the Warden*): You seem different today, Warden. Are you sure everything's OK?

Double: What? (*Pause*) Can he see me? Can he hear me?

Warden: I'm no different today, Russell. Just one day closer to never having to see your face again. In fact, this may be the last time I ever have to see you.

Steven: When's your last day?

Warden: Friday.

Steven: Well, I would say I'll miss you, but that would be lying.

Warden: And you've never told a lie, have you, Russell?

Steven: Never. You leave on Friday, you say? It's a shame it's not a Friday the 13th otherwise I would have waved you off from the parking lot. Since it's not, I suppose I'll just have to wave from here.

Double: I hate him. Hate him!

Warden: You do understand that I've won, don't you?

Steven: Excuse me? Did you say 'won'? I didn't realize we were playing a game, Warden.

Warden: Life is one big game, Russell. You know that. I told you when you first came here that you wouldn't escape while I was in charge.

Steven: You did say that. But what I didn't tell you was that, when we first met, I decided that I didn't want to try and escape again.

The Warden laughs.

Warden: Oh, really?

Double: He's lying! That's exactly what he would say! It's all smoke and mirrors! (*To Steven*) Liar!

Steven (*calmly*): Yes, really. I did decide, however, to throw as much sand in your face as possible.

Warden: It's a good bluff, Russell. But I think we both know otherwise.

Steven: Have they asked you about the film? I'm referring to your friends at the country club?

Double (*to the Warden*): Shoot him! Get a gun from one of the guards and shoot him while we can! We'll say it was an accident. We'll say he was trying to escape! No one could blame us! No one would ever know!

Warden (*calmly*): Nobody's seen your film, Russell. That review in *The Houston Journal* made sure of that. And I've got to tell you, I had to pull quite a few strings to make sure it was written up just the way I wanted.

Narrator (*to Steven*): It was him? He got *The Journal* to give us a bad review?

Warden: I had to offer them a few exclusives with some of your neighbors here on death row, but that's no skin off my nose. That's for the new Warden to worry about.

Steven: Warden, I didn't think you were that sneaky.

Warden: Well, I'm happy to have surprised you.

Steven: It's a shame you couldn't stop them reviewing it positively in every other state though, isn't it? Do you leave Texas often? For vacations, maybe? Where will you be retiring to?

Double (*covering his ears*): Make him be quiet! He's giving me one of my headaches. Make him stop!

Steven: What are you going to do when it comes out on DVD? I think newspapers typically review it again when that happens. You won't be Warden then, will you?

Warden: I'm sure they'll all find it just as dreary as they did the first time.

Steven: Well, look, if this is going to be the last time we see each other I feel like I should give you a retirement gift or something.

Steven picks up one of the reviews and signs it.

So here, have this to remember me by. It's the *New York Tribune* review. You've been to New York, right? Lots of twinkling lights. Liberals everywhere. They loved the film.

The Warden places his hands behind his back. He doesn't accept the review.

Warden: I'll be sure to send you a Christmas card every year, telling you how delicious the ham is.

Steven: I'll look forward to it.

Warden: Goodbye, Russell.

The Warden turns and walks out. The Double doesn't want to leave.

Double: Wait! Come back! (*Pointing*) I think I saw contraband under his pillow! Or in a crack in the wall by the window. Or behind the sink! He's trying to escape, I tell you! He's trying to escape. You can't retire! We need to stay here to make sure he stays behind bars. We should get back in there this instant!

The Double runs out after the Warden, his ranting slowly becoming more distant. The cell door slides closed behind them.

The Narrator turns to Steven and raises his arms in celebration.

Narrator: We did it! By God, we did it!

Steven (*laughing*): Ha ha!

Narrator: Victory tastes so…. Mwah! Deliciously sweet!!!

Steven high-fives the Narrator.

Steven: This was definitely a victory, right?

Narrator (*falling over himself to explain*): Wasn't it clear? We tipped him over the edge! We must have! How else can you explain the appearance of his alter ego, subconscious, or whatever that double of his was?

Steven: You could definitely see him?

Narrator: As clearly as I'm seeing you now.

Steven: I didn't see a thing.

Narrator: Well, trust me he was there. And if you thought the Warden seemed on edge, the other guy was…

The Narrator makes a cuckoo noise.

Steven: He was?

Narrator: Certifiable.

Steven: You thought the Warden seemed on edge?

Narrator: Well, I mean he was trying to hide it, obviously.

Steven: So, do you have to be mad to hear voices and see people that others can't see?

Narrator: Oh, I see where this is going. Well, you couldn't see his double, could you?

Steven: No.

Narrator: Well then, by some strange definition, you're saner than I am.

Steven sits down on his bed.

Steven: I suppose you're right. I don't mean to be a downer. This is a great day. Truly it is. It's what we've been working towards for twelve long years. We did it. And we did it all from this cell. All 12x14x7 feet of it. (*Steven stretches out his arms to hug the Narrator*) Come here.

The Narrator walks over to Steven's bed and embraces. There is an odd metallic, clinking sound.

Narrator (*angrily*): Hey!

When Steven and the Narrator separate, Steven has handcuffed the Narrator to the handrail on the wall next to his bed.

Narrator: What in fuck's name is this?

Steven: This... (*He stands up quickly, checks his watch and then the sliding door behind him*) is goodbye. I'm sorry.

Narrator: What do you mean goodbye? You can't say goodbye to me.

Steven: All good things must come to an end. You know that.

Narrator: And where did you get these cuffs from?

Steven: I took them from Major Linke's utility belt when I gave him the autograph for his nephew.

Narrator: Well, great. I'm going nowhere. Congratulations! But I've got news for you, Einstein: you're not going anywhere either.

Steven: Well, you know, I've been thinking long and hard about that. The way I see it is, there only needs to be one Steven Russell in this cell when the guards come to check on us in (*he checks his watch again*) exactly two minutes...

Narrator: You idiot! They can't see me!

Steven: Can't they? Well, let's test that theory. Now, I don't want you to take this personally, OK? You've helped me a lot over the years. But I kind of think we've outgrown each other, don't you? In many ways, I think I've become more like you. But what I really need now is some me-time. Without you. If you get what I mean.

I need to find out more about this internet malarkey. I want to bank online and buy some crap on eBay. I want to get myself on Facebook and make sure my Wikipedia entry is up to date. I want to Tweet! And drive an electric car. And order a venti white chocolate mocha at Starbucks. I need to spend some time with my daughter and see some of those islands that will soon be under water because of global warming. Who knows, maybe I'll even marry a guy in Massachusetts or some other civilized state.

Narrator: Well that's all lovely, sweetheart, but just how are you going to get out of this cell? Answer me that.

Steven: The same way you always do.

Steven walks over to the edge of his cell, dangles his foot over the edge and then plants it on the stage floor just outside. It's clear he can just walk away.

Steven: Well, how about that?

Narrator: You can't just leave me here!

Steven: What can I say? It's best we go our separate ways. (*He hears someone at the cell door*) Goodbye, my love!

Steven steps off the stage and walks quickly over to Warden Alvarado's office. He watches the Narrator from there.

Major Linke: Roll 24!

Lt. Herrera (*in the distance*): Rolling 24.

The Narrator points at Steven with his free hand.

Narrator: I'm getting away you imbeciles! Wait, what am I saying? He's getting away!

The door slides open and Major Linke comes in followed by Lt. Herrera.

Major Linke: What are you all excited about Russell? Who's getting away?

Narrator (*he points to Steven*): He is! Quick, stop him!

Lt. Herrera: The wall is getting away?

Narrator: Not the wall. Steven Russell!

Major Linke: Really? Steven Russell's getting away, is he? Who are you then? (*He looks at Lt. Herrera and laughs*) His brother?

Narrator: Who am I? That's a good question. (*He looks carefully at both of them*) Obviously, I'm Steven Russell. And you can both see me, right?

Major Linke: Of course, we can both see you.

Lt. Herrera: So who is it that's getting away?

Narrator (*his eyes light up*): An imposter!

Major Linke: An imposter? OK.

Narrator: Look, it's very difficult to explain… (*Calmly*) Actually, I don't think I can explain it. But you're making a terrible mistake.

Lt. Herrera: Russell, I like you. But you need to calm down or I'm going to have to Mace you. OK?

Major Linke: We should just Mace him anyway. I need to pick up a new canister from supplies. This one's almost out. (*He shakes the can to show it's nearly empty*) See?

Over in the Warden's office, Steven waves goodbye to the Narrator, who waves goodbye back.

Lt. Herrera: We can't just Mace him for no reason?

Major Linke: We could say he was playing up.

Steven opens the door to Alvarado's office and walks through, closing it behind him.

Lt. Herrera *(confused)*: Russell? How did you get handcuffed to the wall?

Narrator: Finally, you noticed.

Lt. Herrera *(to Major Linke)*: Did you do that?

Major Linke: No, he was like that when we came in.

Lt. Herrera unlocks the Narrator's handcuffs.

Lt. Herrera: You can't just handcuff someone to the wall and Mace them. What kind of a place do you think this is?

Major Linke: A prison?

Lt. Herrera: Right, and they're the bad guys and we're the good guys. Come on, let's go down to the hall and get something to eat. We were supposed to check on him. We're done. Let's get out of here.

They both turn and leave the cell. The Narrator shakes his head.

Lt. Herrera: Roll 24!

The door to the cell closes. As the guards walk away their voices fade as they walk off stage.

Major Linke: I'm just saying, we're in charge here and it doesn't hurt to show them that every once in a while.

Lt. Herrera: You can't just Mace them. What if they have an allergic reaction or something?

Major Linke: What's with the suit he was wearing?

Lt. Herrera: Maybe he's due in court or something?

The Narrator looks forlornly around his cell and then looks out at the audience.

Narrator: Well, this is a very odd turn of events. You're still here. I suppose that's some consolation. All of a sudden this cell seems smaller than I remember.

He looks down at the letters still all over the floor and sighs.

And it's a mess! I hate mess.

He starts sorting through, ordering and piling up all the letters.

So, I guess we'll be getting a new Warden. Whoever he is, he can't be worse than Alvarado. Although, I'm sure he'll be getting a few phone calls from that guy. Poor man.

He laughs to himself.

You know when you go back and visit your old school, or an old workplace? Or somewhere you once lived. And you look around and you find that nothing's changed since you were last there? It kind of makes you feel good, right? You feel pleased that you can go away, have fun, see new things, and then come back, and it's still the same. Even though you're different. Even though you've changed.

I think I'm that place that doesn't change. I'm the thing that remains constant. You lot can go away on vacation and when you come back, I'll still be here. In this cell, or one like it. You could have a baby, buy a new car, get a new job, go to university, elect a new president or move house, and while you're doing all that... I'll still be here.

Maybe it's for the best, you know? When I think about it. Maybe it's safer. The real world can be a dangerous place. Alvarado's going to have to spend his retirement hoping he never bumps into one of his ex-prisoners down at the local mall. Phillip, if you believe him, is HIV-positive. McVicker, the reporter from *The Houston Journal* who wrote the book, has leukemia. Terri Hodge, the Texan State

Representative who helped me out a couple of times? She was arrested for tax evasion and ended up in prison herself. PhyCor went bankrupt. And that dodgy guy who tried to con John and Glenn? I'm guessing he's still in Mexico or else he's trying to con someone else and having to constantly look over his shoulder.

I can do without all of that drama. My world might be small, but at least it's safe. Which is ironic when you consider I'm on death row, surrounded by a bunch of serial killers and murderers.

Next week, I'll meet the new Warden.

A spotlight highlights Warden Alvarado's office. The Narrator looks over at it.

Narrator: Sally, my daughter, she'll be by to visit me in a few weeks' time.

A second spotlight highlights the visitors' area. The Narrator looks over at it.

Narrator: And I still have the joys of showering and recreation to look forward to every day to get me out of my cell.

A third spotlight highlights the recreation area, minus the cages, center stage.

The Narrator is distracted by a letter he spots on the floor of his cell.

Narrator: That's not an American stamp. I wonder who it's from?

He picks it up, opens it and begins reading.

"Dear Steven,"

"I really enjoyed the movie..." Why, thank you, Laurence. "I also read the book by Steve McVicker..."

Blah, blah, blah.

"Would you be interested in helping me write a play about your life since your final escape and arrest?"

A play? (*He pauses*) Well, that might work.

He picks up his typewriter, feeds in a sheet of paper and starts typing a reply.

"Dear Laurence,"

"Thank you for your letter, which I read with interest. A play sounds like a great idea! I spend most of my days here reading, listening to the radio and generally trying to stay sane. A project like the one you suggest might fit in perfectly with that."

"Rather than answering the long list of questions you include in your letter, might I suggest we start another way? Why don't you come to Texas and visit me so that you can see Gabriel Unit for yourself?"

The spotlight on Warden Alvarado's office goes off.

"That way we'll also be able to size each other up in person."

The spotlight on the recreation area goes off.

"And you'll be able to see with your own eyes what I'm guessing would be the backdrop for our play."

The spotlight on the visitors' area goes off..

The Narrator looks up at the audience from his typewriter.

I'm still here.

Blackout. The End

AFTERWORD

By Steven Russell

WELL HELLO, THERE! IT'S BEEN a long time. Now let me think, the last time I saw you I was looking out from a movie screen and you were snacking on some popcorn and sucking down a Diet Coke. I looked a lot more like Jim Carrey back then. Anyway, you look good. Have you been on vacation recently? Anywhere nice? Somewhere sunny, I bet.

Me? I've been nowhere, done pretty much nothing except read, and hardly seen anyone. Obviously I dabble in this and that. I try to keep myself busy, but there's only so much you can do when you're stuck in a concrete box, seven feet square. Do you want to know what I did today? Well, let me tell you.

Today is a Wednesday. I ate breakfast this morning at 4 a.m. At 5.30 a.m. the two guards working my pod, which is 12 FC 36 for the next two weeks, began their rounds by asking every inmate whether we wanted to recreate and shower today. I took advantage of both opportunities, since today is one of our outside recreation days, and recreated from 6:15 a.m. until about 8:30 a.m. While I've always taken advantage of my daily shower, recreating is something I'm doing more often these days. Until recently my health was remarkably good for my age, which is pretty surprising when you think of everything I've put my body through. My health remains fine, but I know I need to exercise more if I'm to avoid dying in this place.

During recreation, I walked around in circles in an outside rec cage while conversing with a Hispanic inmate in the adjacent cage. We'll call him George. George and I discussed the latest prison drama as well as the national news, family issues and the prison program for ex-gang members (GRAD). George is an ex-Texas Syndicate gang member awaiting transfer to the prison system's gang-renouncement program. Once he completes the program, he'll be released back into general population and out of administrative segregation/death row. I, on the other hand, remain in administrative segregation indefinitely.

After recreation, I was returned to my cell. There I read the newspaper *USA Today* and worked the daily crossword puzzle before being served lunch at 11:15 a.m. After lunch, I read a chapter of Sheldon Novick's biography of the American-born novelist Henry James. I was finally allowed to take my shower at 3 p.m., eleven hours after I ate breakfast. Once I'd cooled off, I hand-washed my boxers and socks in my sink, then dried them on a makeshift clothesline I've constructed from shoelaces bought from the prison commissary. Clothes, towels and sheets must be hand-washed because they always come back dirty from the prison laundry. Why? Because the inmates who work the laundry sell the bleach and detergent to other inmates rather than use it. That twisted logic is prison life in a nutshell.

Throughout the day and into the early evening, I listened to my $20 Chinese radio through a pair of headphones, the cord for which is long enough that I can listen to it while moving about my cell doing other things. I typically begin to focus on the content around 4 p.m. Up until then it's just background noise for me. The programs I listen out for are on *KUHF/Houston Public Radio*, which originates from the University of Houston. During the week I listen to *All Things Considered* from 4-6 p.m., *Classical Music* on *KUHA* from 6-6:30 p.m., *Marketplace* from 6:30-7 p.m. and *The World* from 7-8 p.m.

My supper is usually served to me between 4 p.m. and 6 p.m. Today it came at 4:50 p.m. Mail is usually passed out around 8 p.m., and I'm typically in bed by 9 p.m. Well, I say 'bed', but it's more like those exercise mats your PT teachers made you do forward-rolls on at school. It's not what you'd call cozy, but you'd be surprised what you can get used to when faced with no alternative.

With the exception of weekends, when visitation takes place, every day is basically the same for me. Sunday is the day for haircuts, nail trimming and very early morning showers. There is no recreation in the building on Sundays. I guess because it offends Jesus or something. And that's about it.

It's not what you'd call an action-packed life, is it? Maybe that's why some of the others in administrative segregation or, worse, those awaiting execution, attack TDCJ employees with improvised blades, throw feces at the guards, self-mutilate, take drugs, go mad, and generally misbehave. Not me though. In spite of the minor transgressions detailed here in *Life After Phillip Morris*, I am a saint compared to my neighbors.

Given all I've described above, it should come as no surprise to you that I readily agreed to help when Steve McVicker expressed an interest in turning my life story into a book. His writing gave me a long-term project and provided a welcome distraction from the monotony of daily life. That book ended up being published by Miramax Books and turned into the 2008/9 film *I Love You Phillip Morris*, starring Jim Carrey and Ewan McGregor.

It was during the book-writing/film-making process that the idea of a sequel first occurred to me, something that would cover the drama that ensued after my final arrest and in the years that followed. I shared my idea with McVicker, but, for whatever reason, it didn't seem to resonate with him. I don't think he saw the potential and by then he was increasingly ill with leukemia. Of course, Laurence did see the potential, which is how you're reading this.

I met Laurence through an interview he did for a British magazine. We liked one another and continued corresponding long after our interview was published. Rather than write a sequel as a factual narrative, he wanted to give readers a more movie-like experience since, he reasoned, readers would probably have seen the film. When we met face-to-face in the prison visitation room, in February 2012, we discussed the post-movie possibilities. He pitched his idea to me and a play made perfect sense.

Why did I agree to co-operate with him rather than another writer? Well, after a few months of exchanging letters it was clear to me that he understood and empathized with my situation and the decisions I've made over the years. It's also a hell of a lot easier for someone who's gay to share his or her story with someone else who's gay. No subjects were off limits for us, no question was too personal to ask or answer, and neither one of us took offense at anything the other said or wrote. The result of our co-operation is the book you're holding.

Did you like it? When Laurence sent me a draft to check for inaccuracies, add in some Texan slang, and obtain my blessing, I laughed all the way through. Reading a book or a play about your own life, especially one compiled by someone else, is an experience that I recommend to everyone. I knew from the beginning that he was planning on using an imaginary version of me to create dialogue and narrate the story, but the final result exceeded my expectations. His humor is crude too, just like mine.

How true to life is *Life After Phillip Morris*? Well, I can put my hand on my heart and say that the events in this book happened. Conversations weren't always as they're described, the use of imaginary characters blurs reality with fiction, and the timing and location of events have been altered for dramatic effect... but it all happened. If you're looking for the story of what happened to me after *I Love You Phillip Morris*, this is it.

Let's talk about my mental health. That my character in *Life After Phillip Morris* manifests an imaginary version of himself, as a coping mechanism, implies I'm currently a couple of sandwiches short of a picnic. Certainly, when Warden Alvarado invents his own double at the play's conclusion, we take it as a sign that my character has succeeded in pushing him over the edge. Can the same be said of the real-life me?

Well, prison officials have done an excellent job of affecting my mental state by forcing me to live in a cramped concrete box for almost twenty years. Nowadays my productivity is lower than it used to be, my ability to focus and concentrate is impaired, so much so that I have to read material over and over to absorb it. Letters and essays take me much longer to draft these days. I've been known to mix up my outbound letters in envelopes meant for others, I'm hypersensitive to being around others in close proximity, and often I'll hear my name called by a guard from my cell door, but when I look up no one will be there.

I'm now subject to periodic bouts of paranoia regarding my mail and food e.g. the mailroom is holding my correspondence hostage or the food prepared by the kitchen was done so in an unsanitary manner. I obsessively clean the filthy cells I'm moved into on a biweekly basis, I'm easily distracted and loud noises typically irritate the fuck out of me. Ignoring all the above however, and the fact that I live like a rat in a shoebox, life is just peachy.

What's actually surprising is that I'm not madder than I am. There's a good reason for that of course: I take advantage of every opportunity I can to stay busy, often doing the chores those living outside this concrete box find boring. Why? Because there are no rehabilitative programs for someone like me, held permanently in administrative segregation. So, in order to avoid my own mental breakdown, I'm effectively running my own program. Reading, study and listening to my radio are all helpful in this regard. Additionally, I correspond with more than thirty people from all walks of life, from all over the world. I enjoy hearing about the mundane things they do, their schedules, habits, interests etc., My habits are to stay on a schedule, day after day, and stick to it without fail. Being clean and living in a clean space is my number-one priority after improving the quality of my meals using the various condiments I can source.

Let's discuss why prisons use solitary confinement, shall we? Doubtless, there are some inmates who are a danger to others and should be incarcerated separately and alone. There are still more who are such dangers to society, they should be subject to greater security than a prison's general population. Having seen solitary confinement at first hand however, I can tell you that's not how and why it's being used here in Texas and in other U.S. states. No, solitary confinement is being used to destroy the inmates warehoused therein.

I've known many men who were lucid when they arrived and today can no longer tell you what day or even what year it is. I also know at least fifteen who have committed suicide by hanging, slicing their jugular vein with a piece of plastic or by overdosing on medication. Why do they take their own lives? Well, the isolation makes it impossible for you to be loved by your family and friends since you are literally unable to touch another human being, even during visitation. When you add that to the effect of living in a filthy pod, with chipped paint falling off the walls and ceiling into your food tray, you can understand why some guys simply crack and fold. Even though I'm determined to remain compos mentis, I can still go seventy-two hours without saying a word to anyone here in administrative segregation.

In June 2012, a Senate judiciary subcommittee met to consider the effects of solitary confinement, given that the practice has evolved from being used as a short-term punishment to a routine part of prison management. During the hearing, Senator Richard Durbin, (D-Ill), asked the Director of the Federal Bureau of Prisons whether long-term solitary confinement would have a negative impact on an individual. The Director replied that he "... would have some concerns with prolonged confinement." Durbin's follow-up question should have been, "What then are you doing to end the practice of long-term solitary confinement in U.S. prisons?" Because I can tell you that the TDCJ, to name just one state prison system, doesn't give a damn and hasn't changed its practices in the slightest.

Let me be clear: solitary confinement is totally inappropriate for non-violent offenders like myself. When used in the manner it is today, solitary confinement is torture, pure and simple. Which of course begs the question, should it be banned? My answer to that, perhaps surprisingly, is no. I don't think it should be banned, but I do think it should be used for no more than two years at a time, and only as a behavioral remedy for the most violent offenders. I also believe it should be a matter of policy that during those two years, rehabilitative and vocational programs should be offered to affected inmates. The only reason prison systems get away with what they are doing is because inmates are politically disenfranchised, unorganized, economically disadvantaged and because our communication with the outside world is censored. We are forgotten.

Let me return to talking about this book. Now that you've read *Life After Phillip Morris* what do you think of the title? After discovering that he's no longer part of my life, I know Laurence was reluctant to include Phillip's name when captioning this play. As it is, *Life After Phillip Morris* is an apt title because, in addition to detailing my battles with prison officials, the play describes how Phillip and I fell out of love. In a way, the play is the antithesis of *I Love You Phillip Morris*. It's an anti-love story, if you will. As I write, I haven't heard from Phillip since December 2010, when he told *The Houston Chronicle*, and thus indirectly me, that he was 'one of my victims'. That was news to me.

When Phillip was tried for his part in our NAMM embezzlement, I took the blame for the crime. I testified on Phillip's behalf at his trial, took the blame in the book, proclaimed Phillip's innocence in a letter to his parole panel after he was convicted, told the world's media that he knew nothing about it, and best of all continue to be punished in prison for my part in our crime. When Phillip claimed to be 'one of my victims' he crossed a red line for me, so I no longer feel under any obligation to lie for him or protect him.

So here's what really happened...

My $800,000 NAMM embezzlement began in early 1996 with some bogus invoices created on our home computer in Clear Lake. The bills were for an audit, conducted on various Independent Physician Associations, by a fictional Certified Public Accountant called P.C. Morris. The plan was that, as NAMM's CFO, I would see that the fictitious invoices were paid, and Phillip would pay the resulting checks into his bank account. Phillip was sitting next to me, watching, as the bogus bills were created. At that time, I promised him I would take the blame if anything ever went wrong. When it did, I kept my word. But after reading what Phillip said in that *Chronicle* interview, I don't see why I should any longer. Now he's out on parole there's nothing anyone can do to him by me revealing that he was aware and in complete agreement with the embezzlement plan. He was most definitely not 'one of my victims'.

Nevertheless, in spite of Phillip's betrayal and our estrangement, I have no regrets about meeting him all those year ago. While it's true to say I would never have escaped prison had Phillip not been in my life, it's my belief that had I not fixated on Phillip I would likely have found someone else to obsess over. Obsessive-compulsive disorder, a condition which *Life After Phillip Morris* is right in stating I have been diagnosed with, is a motherfucker.

All that aside, after my last escape, I decided it was time to get my life back under control and stop causing problems for my friends and family. I also came to the realization that Phillip and I would never be together again. I figured that another escape would probably be the straw that broke the camel's back. Had I walked out of here for a fifth time, I don't think they'd ever grant me parole.

Cynics might say that my change in attitude was brought about by the tighter security I was placed under after my fourth escape. For their benefit, let me state that increased security had nothing to do with my decision to give all that up. David Puckett escaped from a facility identical to the one I've been confined to. Had I wanted to pursue a fifth escape, I would have. I have little doubt I would have succeeded. I haven't because I've honestly seen the error of my ways. Life is a lot less stressful not having to sit around scheming about another escape. These days I sleep long and sound every night.

Now allow me to share another of my insights into the U.S. prison system: namely that in America there is one law for the rich and another for the poor. At present, I am very much a member of the latter of these two groups. When America's rich get in trouble they can afford the best legal help money can buy. As such, they will always fare better in our legal system than those without equivalent resources.

Ask yourself how many wealthy men and women are currently in prison serving lengthy sentences? Compare my prison sentence, for example, with that of Jeff Skilling, Enron's former CEO. When Enron became the largest Chapter 11 bankruptcy in U.S. history, shareholders lost more than $60 billion. Skilling was later convicted of conspiracy, insider trading, five counts of making false statements to auditors, and twelve counts of securities fraud. How much prison time was Skilling sentenced to? Twenty-four years and four months. Or, put another way, about 120 years less than me, a man who stole $800,000 and walked out of prison four times. Which one of us has done more damage to society in your opinion?

White-collar crimes and the mismanagement of public funds always seem to go under-punished, in my experience. When PhyCor, the parent company of my former employer, NAMM, filed for bankruptcy in 2002, I was neither surprised nor pleased. I wasn't surprised because the manner in which I was hired demonstrated to me an absence of internal controls at the company. Any company that hires a convicted felon with no accounting experience to run its finance and accounting department probably isn't going to stay in business for very long. Even so, I didn't rejoice when PhyCor went under, in spite of them being the party that pressed charges against me. Why? Because most of the people who lost their jobs at PhyCor when it went bankrupt weren't the ones responsible for its failure. It's always the little guy who suffers.

Since *Life After Phillip Morris* has been written as a play it should, of course, be performed. Will it appear on Broadway? Off Broadway? In London's West End? I hope so. Perhaps theaters will show it as a double-bill alongside *I Love You Phillip Morris*; the film followed by the play? Maybe *Life After Phillip Morris* will itself make it onto the silver screen. Stranger things have happened. I never thought the first half of my life would be made into a film, but that's exactly what transpired after I shared my story with Steve McVicker.

I've never actually seen *I Love You Phillip Morris*. It's one of the first things I'll do if and when I make it out of here. During past media interviews, I'd tell interviewers that other journalists had shown me parts of the film. The aim behind spreading that particular fiction was to make my then Warden wonder how in the world it might be happening. My ploy worked. The Warden in question had the television and VHS/DVD player removed from the officers' muster room in administrative segregation. He then also instructed one of his captains to personally monitor all my remaining interviews. These days I'm much kinder in my dealings with prison officials. I'm less kind with myself however.

In *Life After Phillip Morris* my character tells his daughter he "...doesn't have time for guilt." He says this in the context of missing family birthdays and the like. This is one example of where fact diverges from fiction. Unlike my character in the play, I carry a ton of guilt on my shoulders. I regret missing out on all I have and more. My past behavior was reprehensible and I will continue to pay a price for my actions for the rest of my life. Those who do not carry guilt or have regrets are straight-up sociopaths. There are a few of them around here, but I am not one of them. With a 144-year sentence hanging over me, I've had and continue to have plenty of time to think about the selfish behavior that got me in this fix.

Another aspect of the play I'd like to comment on is the antagonistic relationship between inmates and TDCJ employees. This portrayal is entirely accurate. In real life, prison employees loathe inmates and ninety-five percent of inmates loathe prison employees. Most prison employees are lazy and will typically spend more time trying to get out of doing something than it would have taken just to do it. For example, if I wanted to go outside and recreate with a cute boy on another section of my pod, we'd both have to give up our opportunity to shower. Guards see that as a hassle. If I were to get caught giving another inmate my copy of *USA Today*, the guards working my pod would tell me to give up my shower or else they'd write me a disciplinary case for 'trafficking and trading'. As an ex-cop, this all looks suspiciously like blackmail and bribery, but it's all done to reduce guards' heavy workload. In spite of my celebrity status, TDCJ employees never afford me special treatment. That's fine by me. I never ask for or want anything more than what I'm entitled to.

Since I don't smoke, do drugs or need alcohol, my life is much easier. Why? Well, how do you think those particular items find their way inside the prison system? Plenty of TDCJ employees get terminated every year for bringing in contraband to sell to inmates. Not getting caught up in all that means TDCJ officials have no leverage over me with which to deny me my basic rights. Before I give the whole of TDCJ a bad write-up however, let me state that there are some good TDCJ employees. They are just few and far between.

Why is the conduct of prison staff and the efficacy of our prison system important? Well, in case you hadn't noticed, America is jailing an awful lot of people these days. According to the U.S. Bureau of Justice Statistics (BJS), at the end of 2010 some 2,266,800 adults were incarcerated in federal prisons, state prisons, and county jails. That's about 0.7% of the U.S. population or, put another way, more than the combined populations of Alaska, South Dakota and Wyoming. America is jailing too many people and, as long as retribution and punishment are the driving forces behind putting men and women behind bars, we will always be jailing too many people.

Prison has become a warehouse for the mentally ill and for substance abusers because the 'tough on crime' bigots in the state legislatures and Congress will not appropriate the necessary funds to deal with what's really wrong in these individuals' lives. As it currently stands, the prison system is creating life-long felons out of social misfits. Poor men, disproportionately of Latino and African-American origin, end up coming to prison and learning how to perpetrate more serious crimes than those of which they've been convicted thus far. It makes no sense and it's costing a fortune.

The bigots argue that the prohibitive cost of mass incarceration can be reduced through the use of privately run prisons, which they argue are more efficient and more secure. This is bullshit. The only people for whom private prisons are a good idea are investors, and their existence and expansion fails to address the fact we are jailing too many people in the first place. As for private prisons being more secure, as someone who has escaped prison four times I can tell you now, for free, what is needed is to make prisons more secure. It's not privatizing them. It's a radical idea, but all that's needed is for prison staff to do their jobs. It sounds crazy, right? But I tell you that's all that's necessary. It's the 'try-and-do-everything-not-to-do-my-job' mentality that fosters the trade in contraband, leads to sloppiness and shortcuts and eliminates the strict controls that would otherwise be in place. It's that simple and you heard it here first.

Until we meet again.

Steven J. Russell
January 2018

ABOUT THE AUTHORS

Steven Russell is a four-time prison escapee, fraudster, thief and con-artist, currently serving a 144-year sentence in solitary confinement at the Texas Department of Criminal Justice's Polunsky Unit. He was the subject of the 2009 film *I Love You Phillip Morris*, in which he was portrayed by Jim Carrey. His crimes and prison escapes have also been the subject of documentaries including the *I Almost Got Away With It* series on *Discovery Investigation*, and *The Discovery Channel*'s *On The Run* series. He co-wrote *Life After Phillip Morris* with Laurence Watts, published in 2018.

Laurence Watts is a British-born, American writer, travel writer and editor. He has written for CNN, the BBC, *The Guardian*, *The Huffington Post*, *Pink News*, *Gay Times*, and IR Magazine. He co-edited the final installment of Quentin Crisp's autobiography, *The Last Word*, published in 2017. He co-wrote *Life After Phillip Morris* with four-time prison escapee Steven Russell, which was published in 2018. He studied economics at Queens' College, Cambridge University. He lives in San Diego, California.